Student Guidebook for

COMS 1030

Fundamentals of Public Speaking

Edited by Dr. Angela M. Hosek
Co-Edited by Rebekah P. Crawford
School of Communication Studies
Ohio University | 2016–2017

VAN-GRINER

Student Guidebook for COMS 1030
Fundamentals of Public Speaking

2016–2017
Ohio University
School of Communication Studies
Edited by Dr. Angela M. Hosek
Co-Edited by Rebekah P. Crawford

2016 Copyedited by Sean Gleason
2016 Co-copyedited by Sidi Meyara
Previous copyedit credits to Erin McAloon

About the Internal Photos: Table of Contents—Prosper Tsikata (Ph.D., OU School of Communication Studies) presenting at the School of Communication Studies mini-conference "ComsSubstantiality" in May 2012, photo taken by Li Li (Ph.D., OU School of Communication Studies, COMS 1030 Instructor); Chapter 3—Baker Center, Chapter 12—Alden Library, and OU step photos taken by Jeff Kuznekoff (Ph.D., OU School of Communication Studies); Chapter 1—Schoonover, Chapter 5—Alden Garden, Chapter 6—Rotunda, Chapter 13—Schoonover, Chapter 18—Baker Pond, and cover photos taken by Nate Blazek, OU Undergraduate Student; Cover Photo of the Bricks taken by Chunyu Zhang (OU Doctoral Student); Chapter 4—International Festival Entrance was taken by Valerie Bell Wright (OU Doctoral Student).

Printed in the United States of America
10 9 8 7 6 5 4 3 2 1
ISBN: 978-1-61740-372-9

Van-Griner Publishing
Cincinnati, Ohio
www.van-griner.com

CEO: Mike Griner
President: Dreis Van Landuyt
Project Manager: Hillary Lange
Customer Care Lead: Julie Reichert

Hosek 372-9 Su16
170135
Copyright © 2017

STUDENT GUIDEBOOK FOR COMS 1030
FUNDAMENTALS OF PUBLIC SPEAKING
EDITED BY DR. ANGELA M. HOSEK
CO-EDITED BY REBEKAH P. CRAWFORD

BRIEF CONTENTS

CONTENTS

1 INTRODUCTION TO COMS 1030 AND PROGRAM-WIDE SYLLABUS

2 FACING YOUR FEARS: MANAGING COMMUNICATION APPREHENSION

3 WHO ARE yOU SPEECH ASSIGNMENT

4 PAY IT FORWARD SPEECH ASSIGNMENT

5 IMPROMPTU SPEECH ASSIGNMENT

6 KEEPING IT CLASSY IN COLLEGE:
A NO-NONSENSE GUIDE TO ACADEMIC INTEGRITY

11 INFORMATIVE SPEECH ASSIGNMENT

12 FINDING AND EVALUATING SOURCES

13 APA GUIDELINES

14 ARGUMENT DEVELOPMENT: FRAMING YOUR IDEAS

15 PERSUASIVE SPEECH ASSIGNMENT

16 IMPROMPTU JOB INTERVIEW SPEECH ASSIGNMENT

17 SPEAKING TIPS AND DRILLS

18 COMMUNICATION RESOURCE CENTER INFORMATION

Chapter 1 INTRODUCTION TO COMS 1030 AND PROGRAM-WIDE SYLLABUS

BY DR. ANGELA M. HOSEK
COMS 1030 COURSE DIRECTOR*

*Dr. Laura Black contributed to earlier versions of this chapter.

INTRODUCTION TO COMS 1030

WELCOME

In this class you will learn that public speaking is an important part of civic, professional, and educational life. In COMS 1030 we emphasize that speaking in front of others is important because it is *an opportunity to make a difference* in people's lives. Whether you are speaking in a classroom, a boardroom, a public meeting, an online video, or before an audience assembled for a special occasion, your ability to give a thoughtful and articulate speech can be incredibly powerful.

Public speaking is also at the heart of democracy and is an important foundation of community. In this course we take seriously the idea that good public speaking is not just flashy performances, eloquent phrases, and enticing visual aids. *Speaking in public carries an ethical obligation to be honest, credible, and considerate of your audience.* Good public speaking involves integrity as well as communication skill. Even simple choices like your speech topic, the words you choose, and how you support your ideas have important ethical implications. The assignments in this class invite you to reflect on what is important to you and the communities in which you live. Communicating in public is a privilege and responsibility, and after this class you should be prepared to use your presence in a public forum to make a meaningful difference in your world.

STUDENT GUIDEBOOK OVERVIEW

When you are confident in your message, your goal, your speaking skills, and your ability to relate to your audience, giving a speech can be fun and rewarding. But we recognize that speaking in front of others can also be intimidating. That's why we made this guidebook—to help you develop your ability to speak well in a variety of public settings. This workbook complements your textbook by providing important information about your assignments.

The assignments in this course build on each other to help you develop the knowledge, skills, and confidence you need to be a successful speaker. We begin with smaller speeches that allow you to explore your own ideas and values and get you comfortable speaking in front of a group. Then assignments become more complex. Each one is designed to help you with some aspect of speechmaking. You'll learn to organize your ideas, build arguments, find and evaluate research sources, and create and deliver compelling speeches. Many chapters have tear-out pages (such as worksheets, peer critique forms, and grading rubrics) that you will need to use during the class. Bring the student guidebook and textbook with you to every class.

BUILDING SUCCESS THROUGH PRACTICE, COLLABORATION, AND FEEDBACK

Beyond the particular assignments COMS 1030 offers you an opportunity to learn from one another through feedback and collaboration. There is a lot of important work that happens in this class even when you are not standing in front of the room. Remember that we are all in this together and it is important to respect, help, and support one another throughout the public speaking process.

Each major assignment asks you to work with your peers to practice your speech and give each other feedback. There are workshop days to help you develop your speeches, and on speech day you will each be asked to give written feedback to critique one of your peers. You'll also be asked to go to a public speech that is happening at OU or in your local community and write up a critique. This out-of-class speech critique helps you develop a critical eye for public messages and can help you practice giving good feedback. The workbook provides guidelines to help you with these processes, and your Instructor will help you through these activities. Ultimately, though, it's up to you to make the feedback useful.

To give good feedback, you obviously need to pay close attention to the speaker. But that is not enough—you also need to be supportive and give specific information about both what they did well and what they could improve on. Often students are worried about hurting each other's feelings so they don't want to say anything negative about their friend's speech. Don't fall into this trap! If all of your feedback is vague and positive (like "it was good, I liked it") you are not actually helping your friend get better at speaking. You aren't doing your job. We are here to learn, so please help each other out by taking the critique process seriously. This doesn't mean you should be insensitive. Be supportive and try to offer specific comments. Helpful feedback can include statements like "your introduction really made me interested in your topic" or "your thesis statement was very clear" or "I didn't understand your second main point, can you rephrase it?" or "I got lost during your conclusion because it seemed like your summary wasn't the same as what you actually said in the rest of the speech." All of these can help the speaker see what went well and what specific changes to make to improve the speech.

Receiving feedback can sometimes be difficult. When you listen to a peer critique, remember that your classmate is trying to help you. If he or she is confused by what you say, other audience members might also be confused. Listen to the feedback with an open mind and ask clarifying questions to help you figure out the best way to respond to the critique. It's much better to get good feedback early rather than when you are up on stage giving your speech.

In sum, good public speaking involves a lot of preparation and practice. It also holds great power to shape your social world. For COMS 1030 students, this involves self-reflection, ethical choices, and a serious consideration of things that matter. This guidebook is designed to help you prepare for your assignments and be successful in the class. We look forward to working with you in this course.

PROGRAM-WIDE SYLLABUS

COURSE DESCRIPTION AND OBJECTIVES

The purpose of this class is to teach you theories and skills related to successful communication in the public context. Accordingly, this class is as much a theory class as it is a performance class. In our journey through various theories related to public communication we will explore opportunities for applying these theories in the professional context of our own classroom. After completing this course, you should have accomplished the following objectives:

1 | Define and explain basic communication terms and principles that serve as a basis for competent public communication. (Meets Statewide Outcome #1)

2 | Demonstrate knowledge of concepts related to public communication, including listening, analytical reasoning, verbal communication, nonverbal communication, audience analysis, and research skills. (Meets Statewide Outcome #1, 3, 7)

3 | Research, prepare, and deliver well-organized impromptu, informative and persuasive presentations that contain effective supporting materials and conform to audience members' needs and/or expectations. (Meets Statewide Outcome #2, 3, 4, 6, 7, 8)

4 | Analyze and critically evaluate public communication attempts including speeches delivered by others as well as mass mediated messages. (Meets Statewide Outcome #5, 8)

5 | Apply principles of diversity to public communication situations and demonstrate compete communication practices that respect diverse perspectives. (Meets Statewide Outcome #3)

6 | Locate, analyze, and use research in an ethical manner to support ideas and arguments. (Meets Statewide Outcome #7)

SCHOOL OF COMMUNICATION STUDIES (COMS) MISSION STATEMENT

The School of Communication Studies (COMS) is one of five schools in the Scripps College of Communication. As a school grounded in the Liberal Arts, we seek to equip learners with the knowledge, skills, and abilities to *think critically,* to *make decisions independently,* and to *adapt to an increasingly diverse world.* Our mission is to observe, interpret, and evaluate communication behaviors and processes, with particular interests in the construction of messages and meanings. At both the undergraduate and graduate levels, and across various contexts—interpersonal, organizational, and public—we strive to understand how communication affects *identities, communities,* and *cultures,* and to develop communicators who are *effective* and *ethical.*

REQUIRED TEXTS

This course has two required texts: an e-textbook and a student guidebook. Both are necessary for the successful completion of this course. Most importantly you will complete graded assignments that require your access to the on-line e-textbook.

For this course you will be required to purchase an e-textbook (listed below, hereafter referred to as the textbook) from McGraw-Hill Education Connect. You are not required to have a print textbook, and please be aware if you purchase a used textbook you will still need to purchase Connect access. You can purchase Connect codes in one of the following ways:

- Connect codes are available in the OU bookstores.

OR

- You can purchase directly through McGraw-Hill by opening up your first LearnSmart assignment in Blackboard—this will be Ch. 1 Reading in your COMS 1030 Blackboard. This will launch you in to all the options available to you including *one* of the following options:
    - A redemption of an existing code (that you bought at the bookstore).
    - A two week free trial (you will need to purchase a code after the expiration and all your work will transfer over).
    - Purchase a code with a credit card.
- Also, reference the PowerPoints for step-by-step directions as reviewed by your Instructor and posted on Blackboard.

E-Textbook: Nelson, P., Titsworth, B. S., & Pearson, J. (2013). *iSpeak: Public speaking in contemporary life.* New York: McGraw-Hill.

- E-Textbook ISBN for the Connect Access Code: 9780077493615.

Student Guidebook: A. M. Hosek, & R. P. Crawford (Eds.). (2016). *COMS 1030 fundamentals of pubic speaking: Student guidebook.* Cincinnati, OH: Van-Griner.

- The COMS 1030 Student Guidebook is revised each year and is consumable; therefore, you cannot use previous editions. **The COMS 1030 Student Guidebook can only be purchased from local OU bookstores or at http://store.van-griner.com/content/coms-1030-0.**

CLASS STRUCTURE

This course will be conducted through lecture, discussion, and individual, paired, and group activities. Due to the course objectives and nature of the class, this course is largely performance based. In this course, we will explore the importance of presentational speaking and developing your speaking competencies by engaging in activities that will prepare you to develop, deliver, and evaluate presentational speaking events in your personal, civic, and professional lives. In a cooperative learning atmosphere, students will work individually and collaboratively. This is done so that students can help each other learn and engage with course concepts. This class balances lecture and application of knowledge so that students can express their personal viewpoints and share their experiences as they apply the course concepts. Cooperative learning benefits students because they tend to learn more and retain information better by discussing and applying concepts collaboratively. The experiences students will encounter will increase their awareness of how they communicate, and thus increase their communication competence. This course is also designed to reflect a learner-centered approach, in which students will develop increased confidence and responsibility with regard to their learning and decision making abilities.

COURSE ASSIGNMENTS AND GRADES

The following assignments will be completed by each student. All speaking assignments must be completed in front of an audience to receive a passing grade in the course.

Course Requirements Oral Presentations (53% of Final Grade)	Points	Your Points Earned
1 | Who Are yOU Speech Assignment	20	
2 | Pay It Forward Engagement and Discussion	50	
3 | Impromptu Monologue: Delivery Focus	25	
4 | Informative Speech Assignment	100	
5 | Persuasive Speech Assignment	100	
6 | Impromptu Job Interview Speech Assignment	50	
Analysis Activities (11% of Final Grade)		
7 | Informative Speech Peer Outline Critique	10	
8 | Persuasive Speech Peer Outline Critique	10	
9 | Outside Speech Critique Paper and Class Discussion	50	
Exams (28% of Final Grade)		
10 | Chapter Reading (12 Chapters at 5 points each)	60	
11 | Quizzes (12 at 10 points each)	120	
Participation and Attendance (8% of Final Grade)		
12 | Communication Resource Attendance	30	
13 | COMSTracks Surveys (3 at 5 points each)	15	
14 | Participation in COMS Research	13	
15 | Attendance (refer to policy below)	(add any bonus or subtract any deduction)	
Total Points	**653**	

The following grading scale will be used in the course:

A = 93%–100%   A– = 90%–92%   B+ = 87%–89%   B = 83%–86%   B– = 80%–82%   C+ = 77%–79%

C = 73%–76%   C– = 70%–72%   D+ = 67%–69%   D = 63%–66%   D– = 60%–62%   F = 0%–59%

You can determine your percentage (and grade) by totaling the points you have accumulated and dividing those points by the number of points possible then multiply that number by 100 for your final grade percentage.

COURSE REQUIREMENTS OVERVIEW

ORAL PRESENTATIONS

You will develop and deliver six graded oral presentations. First, you will deliver a Self-Introduction Speech at the beginning of the semester. Next you will deliver the Pay it Forward Speech, which allows you to connect with the community. The third presentation is an Impromptu Speech that will help you focus on your verbal and nonverbal delivery. The fourth presentation features an Informative Speech, and the fifth presentation features a Persuasive Speech. The final Impromptu Speech will occur towards the end of the semester at the discretion of your Instructor. Assignment descriptions, evaluation criteria, evaluation forms, and other associated documents for each assignment are located in the COMS 1030 Student Guidebook.

ANALYSIS ACTIVITIES

Peer Critiques

During the Informative and Persuasive Speech assignments you will do peer critiques that allow you to engage in feedback sessions with your classmates. Your Instructor will provide additional information about how these critiques will be conducted.

Out-of-Class Speech Critique

You will attend a formal-type speech outside of class and write a three-page analysis of the speech using concepts, ideas, and theories from your text and class discussion. The assignment description, evaluation criteria, evaluation forms, and other associated documents for this assignment are located in the COMS 1030 Student Guidebook.

CONTENT MASTERY

Chapter Reading

You will read the course e-textbook chapters online and engage in adaptive reading and practice exercises to ensure you understand, comprehend, and can apply course concepts. You will have the opportunity to master 12 chapters by (a) reading the chapter **and** (b) engaging in the practice comprehension activities as you read. **You must complete the reading and practice comprehension activities by the due dates specified in the Semester Schedule to earn 100% completion.** For each chapter you complete 100% you earn 5 points. If you do not complete the entire chapter and comprehension activities you will receive a percentage for whatever you did complete out of the 5 points. The *Chapter Reading* process ensures you are reading and processing material as we are applying it in class. You will find the readings for each chapter through the *Chapter Reading* tab on Blackboard.

Quizzes

You are expected to read textbook chapters as assigned on the *semester schedule* and be prepared to discuss and work with the material in class. Engaging in the *Chapter Reading* discussed above will, in part, help you achieve this goal. To assess your understanding, comprehension, and application of our course content you will take 12 quizzes over the course of the semester (due dates are listed in the *Suggested Semester Schedule*). **All quizzes will be timed at 30 minutes and once you begin the quiz you will have to take it in its entirety.** Quizzes will not be reopened unless an extreme circumstance occurs. Since the quizzes are online you have access to the quizzes 24/7, until the deadline.

*The quizzes are designed for self pacing. You can take the quizzes weekly as we work with the content (this is our recommendation) or you can do them in larger chunks. All quizzes are open at the start of the semester so you can move on pace or faster if you'd like *but* quizzes close **on the dates listed in the *Semester Schedule*** and will not reopen once they close.

CLASS PARTICIPATION AND ATTENDANCE

You are expected to take an active part in class discussions. This includes reading assignments and engaging in classroom activities. Throughout the course, your Instructor will assign various activities to help facilitate learning of course concepts. In addition, the following activities will factor in to your course grade.

Attendance

COMS 1030 is a performance-based course that emphasizes experiential learning as well as cognitive learning; therefore, it is important that you attend every class. Attendance will be factored into your final course grade. Your attendance is not only important to your own success, but also to that of your class community, as you will provide feedback to your peers during their speeches. A record of attendance will be kept for each student through daily sign in sheets that require your signature.

Bonus Attendance Points

If you have perfect attendance (meaning you have physically attended every class) and your attendance is punctual (see Late Arrival/Leaving Early policy), **10 bonus points** will be added to your final point total at the end of semester.

The COMS 1030 Program recognizes excused absences for documented university sponsored travel and for Religious Observances (see policy below) and for extreme and dire personal emergencies. As per the Student Handbook excused absences **with documentation** include death in the immediate family, documented illness, religious observance, jury duty, and involvement in Ohio University-sponsored activities. It is your responsibility to provide documentation. Meetings for other classes, appointments with advisors, work excuses, and many other personal reasons for missing class are not considered "excused" absences. Generally, absences equaling the number of times a given class meets in one week will not adversely affect your grade. Below are the guidelines for all COMS 1030 courses:

- For classes that meet three times each week (M/W/F), your first three absences are without penalty.
- For classes that meet two times each week (M/W or T/TH), your first two absences are without penalty.
- For classes that meet one time each week (evening classes), your first absence is without penalty.

You can use these penalty-free absences as insurance for times of unforeseen circumstances.

Absences **beyond** the specified number listed above will result in your final course grade being lowered 10 points for <u>each</u> additional absence. For example, if you are on a T/TH schedule and you miss a total of four classes (two are without penalty) your final grade points will be lowered by 20 for the additional two absences. Any student missing more than 1/3 of the class periods for any reason should withdraw and re-take the class; those missing more than 1/3 of the class periods will not be awarded a passing grade in the course.

Late Arrival/Leaving Class Early

Punctuality is vital to our course, especially during speech days. We define punctuality as being no more than five minutes late at the beginning of class and remaining until class is dismissed. Therefore, unless otherwise approved by your Instructor for extreme circumstances, arriving to class late and/or leaving class early (in any combination) will result in an absence each time upon the third occurrence. For example, 3 late arrivals = 1 absence; 3 late arrivals and leaving early 3 times = 2 absences and so on.

COMSTRACKS SURVEYS

What Is the Purpose of These Surveys?

The COMS 1030 Program engages in semester-long progress activities that require your involvement. These surveys are part of an ongoing analysis of the COMS 1030 Program curriculum.

When Will They Happen?

Three times during the semester (beginning, middle, and end), you will be contacted via email by our COMS 1030 Program Director, Dr. Angela M. Hosek, with information about these surveys and links to access them online using Qualtrics.com. The time-frames for these assessments appear on the *Semester Schedule*.

What Are the Surveys About?

In general, you will be asked about your feelings and perceptions about communicating in and about various speaking contexts and about your experiences in COMS 1030. These will include questions about communication apprehension, your preparation for speeches, perceptions about our course curriculum, and your specific COMS 1030 class. The goal with these assessments is to examine students' progress and continually improve our course. Your feedback is vital to this process. We take these assessments very seriously and we hope you will too.

How Do These Assessments Factor in to My COMS 1030 Grade?

Each assessment is worth 5 points of your total course grade (total of 15 points) and earned solely for your participation **not** on the quality of your response. In other words, for each survey you complete in its entirety you receive the points. Each assessment will have specific access periods during which each must be completed. Towards the end of the semester, Dr. Hosek will notify your Instructor of the total points you earned for each assessment. Your responses will be kept confidential and any identifying information will be removed before any analyses are conducted. Your Instructor will provide more details about these assessments throughout the semester.

RESEARCH PARTICIPATION REQUIREMENT

You will earn (2%) of your course grade by either participating in a research study or completing the alternative assignment (a journal article summary). To complete this requirement, register on the Communication Studies Research Participation System (CSRPS), *http://ohio-coms.sona-systems.com/,* during the first two weeks of the term and complete a prescreening questionnaire, worth 3 points (0.5%). At that time, you can choose to participate in a research study **or** to complete the alternative assignment (both are worth 9 points, or 1.5%). If you choose to participate in a research study, you will be assigned to a specific study. The researcher for that study will contact you about your participation. If you choose to complete the alternative assignment, the instructions for the assignment are available on the CSRPS. Additional information is available on the COMS website (*http://www.coms.ohiou. edu/*). Please note that this assignment is **not** extra credit, but is part of your course credit. You will need to complete a separate research study or alternative assignment for each Communication Studies class that requires a research experience. Questions about the research requirement should be directed to: coms-research@ohio.edu.

COMMUNICATION RESOURCE CENTER (SCHN 030)

As part of your enrollment in COMS 1030 you have access to the Communication Resource Center (CRC). You will attend the CRC at least once as part of your COMS 1030 grade for 30 points. This center features a lab where you can go for help to prepare and enhance your oral communication skills in a positive, friendly, and safe environment with trained COMS 1030 Peer Leaders. For your appointment you can work on topic selection, outlining, research advice, and perhaps most importantly engage in a filmed recording of your presentation and engage in a constructive feedback sessions with a Peer Leader. Doing so will allow you take full advantage of the resources in the CRC. The center is located at SCHN 030. To schedule your 20-minute appointment go to *http:// comsspeechlab.appointy.com/.* We also plan to have walk-in and extended hours during major speech timelines. Provide your Instructor with the feedback form from the CRC Staff to obtain your 30 points. More information on specific CRC times will be shared during the semester. You can also email the CRC Coordinator at speechlab@ ohio.edu.

*Your documented attendance at the CRC serves as your grade for that portion of our course (e.g., 30 points) and it can improve your presentation grades in COMS 1030. That said, the feedback you receive in the CRC is to be used for your own development and practice and does not inform the grades you earn on any work in COMS 1030.

COURSE POLICIES

Academic Misconduct Policy

Academic misconduct includes traditional textual plagiarism and its manifestations, including self-plagiarism, falsifying work or academic records, cheating, substitution of work for the work of another, actively participating in or condoning these activities with others, appropriating creative works of art in whole or part (images, sounds, lighting designs, audio tracks, scripts, etc.). Students who are uncertain of what constitutes acts of Academic Misconduct should talk to their Instructor(s) and refer to the most recent edition of the OU's Policy on Academic Misconduct *http://www.ohio.edu/communitystandards/academic/index.cfm*.

Plagiarism means representing the words or ideas of another person as your own. This includes quoting or paraphrasing from published sources without acknowledging/citing the source of your information and/or presenting quoted material as your own words. Students who are unfamiliar with how to cite sources should purchase a style manual such as APA (American Psychological Association). Claiming a lack of knowledge about standards for writing is not an acceptable excuse for committing plagiarism.

In cases of academic misconduct the *Instructor* and COMS 1030 Director will determine appropriate academic sanctions, which may include anything ranging from re-doing the assignment to an automatic failing grade in the course. Students disagreeing with the academic sanctions may go through the standard grade appeal process followed by the School of Communication Studies. In addition to the academic sanctions, all instances of academic misconduct, regardless of severity, are referred to OU's Office of Community Standards and Student Responsibility. OU's Office of Community Standards and Student Responsibility may impose additional sanctions; however, that process is separate from the academic sanctions enforced by your Instructor and COMS 1030 Director and will have no impact on the grade assigned in COMS 1030. Please refer to the Student Handbook for a discussion of the penalties for plagiarism, cheating, and other forms of academic misconduct. Such information may be found at: *http://www.ohio.edu/communitystandards/*.

Own your own words and your voice and this comes from doing you own creative, innovative, and original work.

SafeAssign Policy

In an effort to help prevent plagiarism in COMS 1030 and at Ohio University, our section will be using a service called SafeAssign, which is a part of Blackboard for all written work. SafeAssign is a service that helps prevent plagiarism by detecting possible unoriginal content and generating a report viewable by instructors. All typed assignments must be submitted to SafeAssign. **Hard copies will not be accepted for a grade.** More information about SafeAssign can be found your Blackboard page from your Instructor.

Policy on Late Work

All graded work is due on the dates specified in the "Suggested Semester Schedule." You are expected to be present in class and prepared on those dates. Generally, graded work will not be accepted after the due date. Only under the most extreme circumstances will late work be accepted, and even under those circumstances a penalty of 10 points per class session may be assessed. All late work will be due the following class period unless otherwise determined by your Instructor in coordination with the COMS 1030 Director. If work is not submitted the next class period it cannot be turned in. This policy refers to all coursework except the actual delivery of a speech (see policy on Missed Speeches for information on late speeches).

Written Work Expectations

You are expected to turn in high-quality written work. In particular, it is expected that you have proofread all written work for spelling and grammatical errors. **If these steps have not been taken, your Instructor reserves the right to refrain from grading the written work and you may be asked to re-write the assignment with a deduction of up to 10 points.** It is well within your control to turn in your best work. Please visit the Student Writing Center (SWC) Alden Library, 2nd Floor, 740-593-2646 or email writingcenter@ohio.edu for assistance.

Special Needs Accommodation

We are happy to accommodate any special needs you may have throughout the class. If you have need for accommodation we encourage you to contact the Student Accessibilities Services (SAS) office 740-593-2620 or email disabilities@ohio.edu. Although we try to accommodate students whenever possible, we require written documentation from SAS for ongoing accommodations.

Commitment to Social Justice

OU is committed to fostering a climate of respect for students, faculty, and staff, as well as others who participate in the University's programs and activities. Every student in this class will be honored and respected as an individual with distinct experiences, talents, and backgrounds. Students will be treated fairly regardless of race, religion, sexual orientation, gender identification, disability, socio-economic status, or national identity. Issues of diversity may be a part of class discussion, assigned material, and projects. The Instructor will make every effort to ensure that an inclusive environment exists for all students. If you have any concerns or suggestions for improving the classroom climate, please do not hesitate to speak with your Instructor, the COMS Director, or to contact the Office of Diversity and Inclusion at 740-593-2431 or by email diversityinclusion@ohio.edu.

We expect to maintain a learning culture based upon open communication, respect, inclusion, and non-discrimination. As such, OU and all of us involved in COMS 1030 expect its students, faculty, staff, and other members of the OU Community will conduct themselves appropriately and refrain from behavior that infringes on the rights of others. It is the responsibility of COMS 1030 personnel and their students to uphold these commitments.

Student Guidebook, Blackboard, Email, Twitter, and General Software Access

The COMS 1030 Student Guidebook, textbook, email, and Blackboard are essential for this course. The syllabus, all assignments, and other main course materials are located in the Student Guidebook. Your Instructor will provide a Semester Schedule and may provide a supplement to this syllabus that clarifies their expectations and policies for organizing class sessions (the supplement does not modify/change/supersede the program-wide syllabus). We recommend that you check your email and Blackboard once a day. Your Instructor will use email and Blackboard to provide course and grade information.

> The COMS 1030 Program has a Twitter account that we will use to publicize upcoming speaking events and communication related news. It's also a space for all COMS 1030 sections and Instructors to interact!
>
> Follow on Twitter
> @COMS1030_OU
>
> **COMS 1030 IS ON TWITTER!**
> **@COMS1030_OU**

You can access the course Blackboard page as a student enrolled in this class from any on-campus or off-campus computer through the OU webpage.

In general, any COMS 1030 course documents placed on Blackboard will be available in Microsoft WORD and/ or Acrobat PDF format. If you do not have personal access to these programs, you can access them using any OU computer lab. Your Instructor will inform you of any additional software required (e.g., Microsoft PowerPoint).

Missed Speeches/Prolonged Absence

If you should miss class on a day when you are scheduled to present or during impromptu speech days you must get in contact with your Instructor *before class* to discuss your absence. Failing to make contact with your Instructor before class *will result in a zero grade for that speech assignment*. Only under the most extreme circumstances can speeches be delivered late, and even under those circumstances points may be deducted based on the discretion of your Instructor in coordination with the COMS1030 Director. In any case of prolonged absence (more than a week) due to an accident or illness, you should immediately notify the Dean of Students and your Instructor(s).

COMS 1030 FEEDBACK

As a student enrolled in this course, your constructive feedback is important. If you have feedback, concerns, problems, recommendations, and/or positive experiences/highlights related to COMS 1030, please share them with the Program Director, Dr. Angela M. Hosek, at hosek@ohio.edu or stop by for a visit in SCHN 403 during office hours. *Discussions regarding daily class operations, management, and student performance should first be discussed with your individual COMS 1030 Instructor.*

Chapter 2 FACING YOUR FEARS: MANAGING COMMUNICATION APPREHENSION

BY VALERIE RUBINSKY

FACING YOUR FEARS | MANAGING COMMUNICATION APPREHENSION

You may be familiar with Jerry Seinfeld's famous quote, "According to most studies, people's number one fear is public speaking. Number two is death. Death is number two. Does that sound right? This means to the average person, if you go to a funeral, you're better off in the casket than doing the eulogy" (as cited in Titsworth & Peterson, 2014). Seinfeld's joke alludes to what Communication Studies scholars have long called Communication Apprehension (CA). This chapter will highlight some of the extensive research about CA, the effects of CA, and outline strategies for succeeding in this course if you find yourself having anxiety surrounding the specific context of presentational/public speaking.

COMMUNICATION APPREHENSION, WILLINGNESS TO COMMUNICATE, AND STAGE FRIGHT

Communication Apprehension

Research considers communication apprehension (CA) a "broad-based fear or anxiety associated with either real or anticipated communication with another person or persons" (McCroskey, 1976, p. 1). CA is considered the single-most researched construct in the field of communication studies (Wrench, Brogan, McCroskey, & Jowi, 2008). Broadly, it exists in four basic contexts: interpersonal, meeting, group, and public (Wrench et al., 2008). This means people might experience CA when speaking in front of large groups, small groups, or even one-on-one. In these basic contexts, CA presents itself as either a trait, in a generalized context, with a particular individual or group across varied contexts, or with a given individual or group in a particular situation (McCroskey, 1982; Wrench et al.).

CA affects at least 20 percent of people (Hart, 2005; McCroskey & Richmond, 1979). An individual can have high or low trait-like CA. CA is trait-based, but can also be state-based. CA is rooted in a real or anticipated fear. Trait-like CA is more than experiencing anxiety about a specific communication event like giving a speech in front of your class because the apprehension does not pass when the communication event ends (McCroskey, 1998). Whereas, state-based CA refers to anxieties that are dependent on the situation. In the presentational speaking sense, we typically think of state-CA as stage fright (Kearney, McCroskey, & Nimmo, 1980), which you'll read more about in the next section. While someone who does not experience high trait-like CA generally expects a positive, rewarding experience as a result of communication interactions, someone with high trait-like CA will anticipate punishment (or lack of reward) from their communication experience (McCroskey, 1998). Importantly, CA describes how people *feel* about communication rather than how they actually *communicate* (Honeycutt, Choi, & DeBerry, 2009; McCroskey, Richmond, Berger, & Baldwin, 1983).

Additionally, experiencing high levels of trait-like CA may hinder public speaking performance, but having high trait-like CA does not necessarily mean performance will suffer. In fact, CA can sometimes help focus and improve communication (Honeycutt et al., 2009), and students enrolled in public speaking courses with the highest CA show the largest improvement in perceived public speaking competence (Titsworth & Pearson, 2014). Problems tend to occur when people experience "chronically" high levels of CA (Honeycutt et al., p. 239). CA is not associated with age, assigned sex, or GPA (Titsworth & Pearson).

Stage Fright

Additionally, it is important to clarify the distinction between CA and stage fright. Stage fright refers to the fear or anxiety associated with participation in a *public* performance or anticipation of that participation (McCroskey, 1976). To some degree, stage fright is experienced by nearly everyone. In contrast, CA is a response to "any real or anticipated communication experience, either public or private, with any number of other people" (McCroskey, p. 2). Certainly, someone who is high in CA will also experience a more stressful response to communication in a public setting (like public speaking), but someone who simply experiences stage fright probably will not experience the same anxiety for every other type of communication experience that they do for public speaking. For example, while someone who experiences stage fright might be nervous before giving a speech, they probably will not feel the same anxiety before answering a phone.

Willingness to Communicate

Importantly, CA and stage fright are not the same as the personality orientation of willingness to communicate (WTC). WTC refers to a person's *preference* to initiate or avoid communication, so whether or not you like communicating (McCroskey, 1998). You may not *like* to communicate or may not *like* public speaking but you do not necessarily have a fear of it. However, people with high trait-like CA tend to also be low in their willingness to communicate (McCroskey, 1998).

Effects and Symptoms of CA

Research finds that people with high CA also tend to have low self-image. Further, very high CA affects housing and career choices, daily group interactions, and social choices (McCroskey, 1976). CA can interact with other social phobias, which we call social communication apprehension (SCA; Wrench et al., 2008).

Symptoms of CA may include sleeplessness, worry, reluctance prior to a presentation, and off-task thoughts while presenting (Titsworth & Pearson, 2014). Additionally, people high in CA tend to focus on dry mouth, sweaty palms, and shaky legs present during public speaking (Titsworth & Pearson). When students high in CA take a public speaking course, they tend to be less concerned with audience adaptation, have difficulty identifying content for a speech, and experience more self-doubt about their speaking abilities (Titsworth & Pearson, 2014). However, research tells us that experiencing very low CA may also cause trouble in public speaking, so both very high and very low CA may be problematic (Honeycutt et al., 2009). For people high in trait-like CA, this may be a part of who you are, and that's okay, but there is hope for managing it when you have to give presentations. The next section will offer some tools you can use to manage CA and even thrive in those situations.

CA REDUCTION STRATEGIES AND THRIVING IN 1030

Four major reduction strategies emerged throughout the extensive body of research on CA: skills training, rational emotive therapy, systematic desensitization, and cognitive modification and visualization (Honeycutt et al., 2009; Ayres & Hopf, 1987). The remainder of this chapter will focus on steps that you can take to help reduce your CA or stage fright, specifically steps you can take yourself or that your COMS 1030 Instructor and the Communication Resource Center (CRC) can help you with while you are in this course.

Visualization and Imagined Interactions

Visualization, which has a pretty high success rate (Ayres & Hopf, 1987), involves being able to imagine yourself having a successful performance prior to the communication experience. Before you give your speech, visualize yourself successfully giving the speech. Similarly, imagined interactions provide another way to reduce anxiety associated with communication by imagining the anticipated communication experience and imagining it positively. Imagined interactions are described as the process of "social cognition whereby actors imagine and therefore indirectly experience themselves in anticipated and/or past communicative encounters with others" (Honeycutt, 2003, p. 2). Choi, Honeycutt, and Bodie (2015) argue that you can directly affect your own CA or anxiety by "experiencing a future conversation" through your own imagination (p. 26).

Affirming Thoughts

Simply put, think positive. Most likely, you do not look as nervous as you think you do. Your audience probably can't tell if your hands are shaking, or if you forgot a detail. Act as if you are confident standing in front of the class, and tell yourself you are going to perform confidently and well. Negative self-talk (Fassl & O'Beirne, 1995; Fremouw & Scott, 1979; Titsworth & Pearson, 2014) is one way that CA manifests. Identifying and correcting these disaffirming thoughts will help reduce your anxiety. Similarly, focusing on your strengths rather than your shortcomings will help correct problematic thought patterns that lead to speaking anxiety (Fremouw & Scott; Fassl & O'Beirne).

Audience as Allies

We are all in this together! Remember, most people experience some degree of stage fright. Your classmates care about how you do in your presentation (Titsworth & Pearson, 2014). Your classmates are your allies, and in 1030 you are learning and growing as speakers together. Look at your audience and focus on those members of your audience that make you feel good—the people who are nodding or smiling. This relates to those affirming thoughts we talked about earlier. Tell yourself that your audience is on your side and wants you to succeed, that they are rooting for you, and that they care about you. This perception will impact your anxiety and performance (Titsworth & Pearson).

Your Subject

In COMS 1030, you are in the unique position to speak about something you should know and care about. Knowing and caring about your subject are potential ways to reduce anxiety associated with public speaking (Titsworth & Pearson, 2014). Being able to speak about a subject with passion is one way to channel those nerves associated with stage fright in a positive way. Additionally, do your homework. You have likely heard your 1030 teacher say that "the best way to sound like you know what you're talking about is to know what you're talking about." There is no substitute for doing the work. If you know your subject well, it will be easier to recall details under pressure.

Practice Makes Perfect

Similarly, there is no substitute for practice. You would not expect to ace an exam that you didn't study for, so you should not expect to give an excellent speech if you have not rehearsed it. Lack of preparation for a speech is a rational anxiety, like the fear you might experience taking a final exam for which you did not study. The best way to manage that fear is to appropriately prepare. This includes practice. Gradually working up to the big speech is a way to manage those nerves.

- First, practice by yourself out loud.

- Then, practice in front of someone you trust—a friend, a roommate, a family member, a partner, or whoever makes you feel comfortable.

- Then, try practicing in front of a small group.

Practice should be part of the preparation process for your 1030 speeches anyway, so take advantage of that process to gradually increase the exposure to the public speaking setting. If you especially experience high CA, this may even affect the preparation process (McCroskey, 1982). In cases where you are too nervous to practice even by yourself or in front of a roommate, you should speak to your public speaking Instructor about your CA.

Finally, take care of yourself. Public speaking related fears are real anxieties, but you are in an environment to work through them this semester with access to resources and support including the CRC. Attend the CRC to practice presenting your speech and get feedback from your peers who recently took COMS 1030! You can also go there to work on topic selection, outlining, research suggestions, impromptu, and delivery practice. The trained peer staff and the CRC Coordinator are there to help you. Plus it is part of your grade to attend at least once! Additionally, the university counseling services, your classmates, and your Instructor are valuable resources to help you as you prepare. Finally, take care of yourself—get enough sleep and do not give a speech on an empty stomach. CA and stage fright are common and you are not alone in experiencing them. Engage in positive self-talk, do your research, practice, and see your classmates as allies to help manage anxiety associated with public speaking.

Key Take-Aways

- CA is broad-based anxiety associated with communication interactions.

- Stage fright is a specific type of communication apprehension associated with public communication performances, and is experienced by most people to some degree.

- Ways to manage stage fright and CA before your speech include doing your research, gradually practicing in front of more and more people, and engaging in positive and affirming self-talk and visualizing positive speaking outcomes.

- Ways to manage these anxieties during your speech include avoiding negative self-talk or thinking of yourself as a failure for minor slip ups, viewing the audience as friends and allies, and focusing on people giving you positive non-verbal feedback.

- Attend the CRC for support and practice.

REFERENCES

Ayres, J., & Hopf, T. S. (1987). Visualization, systematic desensitization, and rational emotive therapy: A comparative evaluation. *Communication Education, 36*(3), 236–240.

Choi, C. W., Honeycutt, J. M., & Bodie, G. D. (2015). Effects of imagined interactions and rehearsal on speaking performance. *Communication Education, 64*(1), 25–44. doi:10.1080/03634523.2014.978795

Fassl, J., & O'Beirne, B. (1995). Communication apprehension intervention: A report of a spring 1995 pilot study program utilizing self-Esteem measures and cognitive restructuring as intervention strategies for high CA students in the basic course.

Fremouw, W. J., & Scott, M. D. (1979). Cognitive restructuring: An alternative method for the treatment of communication apprehension. *Communication Education.*

Hart, H. (2005). Engineering communication: Overcoming speech anxiety. Retrieved from The University of Texas at Austin, CE 333T: Engineering Communication Website: http://www.ceutexas.edu/prof/hart/33t/anxiety.cfm.html

Honeycutt, J. M., Choi, C. W., & DeBerry, J. R. (2009). Communication apprehension and imagined interactions. *Communication Research Reports, 26*(3), 228–236. doi:10.1080/08824090903074423

Kearney, P., McCroskey, J. C., & Nimmo, D. (1980). Relationships among teacher communication style, trait and state communication apprehension and teacher effectiveness. *Communication Yearbook, 4,* 533–551.

McCroskey, J. C. (1976). The problems of communication apprehension in the classroom. *Florida Communication Journal, 4*(2), 1–12.

McCroskey, J. C. (1998). *An introduction to communication in the classroom.* Acton, MA: Tapestry Press.

McCroskey, J. C. (1982). *An introduction to rhetorical communication* (4th Ed). Englewood Cliffs, NJ: Prentice-Hall.

McCroskey, J. C. (2009). Communication apprehension: What have we learned in the last four decades. *Human Communication, 12*(2), 157–171.

McCroskey, J. C., & Richmond, V. P. (1979). The impact of communication apprehension on individuals in organizations. *Communication Quarterly, 27,* 55–61.

Titsworth, S., & Pearson, J. C. (2014) *iSpeak.* New York, New York: McGraw-Hill.

Wrench, J. S., Brogan, S. M., McCroskey, J. C., & Jowi, D. (2008). Social communication apprehension: The intersection of communication apprehension and social phobia. *Human Communication, 11*(4), 409–429.

Chapter 3 WHO ARE YOU SPEECH ASSIGNMENT

BY DR. ANGELA M. HOSEK
COMS 1030 COURSE DIRECTOR

WHO ARE yOU SPEECH ASSIGNMENT

ASSIGNMENT OVERVIEW

(20 points)

Think about the last time you introduced yourself to someone at work, at school, or in a local hangout. Now think about the last time someone introduced themselves to you. These introductions can typically follow the same script and are often factual accounts of roles we have or brief accounts of places we've been. Typically, they lack dynamism and leave you or the other person not really feeling like you know "who they/you are." For this low-stakes assignment we are going to flip the script and create a dynamic self-introduction.

To get a better sense of this, watch this YouTube video on *https://www.youtube.com/watch?v=pXbs8N5e3mg.*

ASSIGNMENT GUIDELINES AND REQUIREMENTS

Each student will create and deliver a three-minute informative presentation that provides a narrative self-introduction.

WHAT IS THIS SPEECH ABOUT?

You have two goals for this speech:

1 | **The y in yOU** in the title of this speech is about YOU. Introduce yourself in a way that helps your audience remember your unique personal identity in a similar way to how the speaker did in the Youtube video. Don't just list facts ... help your classmates get to know who you are in a memorable way. This *may* include sharing aspects of your identity like where you are from, your interests, major/minor, or hobbies. Think about what it feels like when you meet a new group of people and what makes you remember some people over others and use what you've seen those people do well to help your audience learn more about you.

2 | **The OU in yOU** reminds us that we are all part of a shared identity as members of the Ohio University culture. As you share parts of who you are, if it makes sense, you can also share something about how OU relates to who you are.

OUTLINE

Although we have not discussed speech outlines and organization at this point in the semester, it will be beneficial for you to begin working with these processes. As you create your introduction it will be helpful to create a mini outline to ensure you are thinking of structuring your ideas in similar ways that reflect how the YouTube speaker engaged us in the revised introduction. We are purposely being loose with the guidelines here to allow you some creativity and innovativeness.

DELIVERY AND NOTES

Since this is your first presentation and we have yet to discuss outlining and delivery, you should practice your introduction but also be informal and casual since this is a chance for us to get to know each other. **This is intentionally a low stakes assignment worth 20 points of your grade.**

PRESENTATION FEEDBACK

You will receive feedback from your Instructor for this presentation. This feedback will help you prepare for upcoming graded assignments and, more importantly, provide you with insight as to how your audience perceives your presentational speaking strengths and where they see opportunities for improvement.

WHO ARE yOU FEEDBACK FORM

Speaker's Name: _____ Total Points: _____ /20

Time Infraction: _____ Time: _____

General Assignment Guidelines (check all items that were completed).

☐ Speech met criteria of assignment (time limit, integrated self-introduction modeling example YouTube video style).

☐ Topics discussed were relevant to assignment guidelines.

☐ Attempts were made to follow an organizational structure.

☐ Attempts at effective verbal (e.g., clarity, concise, pronunciation, articulation) and nonverbal delivery (e.g., eye contact; vocal variety; movement; and, if necessary, gestures).

Presentational Strengths:

Opportunities for Improvement:

Speeches have a 15 second grace period over/under time limit without penalty. Speeches that go 16–29 seconds over/under the time limit will be reduced by 3 points. Speeches that go 30 seconds over/under the time limit will be reduced by 5 points. Excessive time infraction can result in larger penalty per discretion of Instructor.

Chapter 4 PAY IT FORWARD SPEECH ASSIGNMENT

ADAPTED BY STEVIE MUNZ*

*This assignment was adapted from Mckenna-Buchanan, T. & Munz, S. (2014). *The Pay It Forward Speech: Challenging students to become engaged in the community. Communication Teacher, 28,* 177-182. doi 10.1080/17404622.2014.911337

PAY IT FORWARD SPEECH ASSIGNMENT

ASSIGNMENT RATIONALE

This speaking assignment provides you with an opportunity to *pay it forward* to three different people in the community and share your experiences with your classmates in a round table discussion format. You are instructed to perform three *pay it forward acts* or unconditional acts of kindness. Students will also construct a speech outline and develop speaking skills by reflecting on unconditional acts of kindness.

BACKGROUND

The premise of the novel and motion picture *Pay It Forward* (2000) is that any person can implement an act of kindness in his or her own life. An act of kindness begins with doing a favor for another person without any expectation of being paid back. The unconditional favors can be large or small. As the fictional main character, 12-year-old Trevor observes, "It doesn't have to be a big thing. It can just seem that way, depending who you do it for."

ASSIGNMENT GUIDELINES AND REQUIREMENTS

Overview

Each student will:

1 | Perform three *pay it forward acts* of kindness and construct an outline.

   The pay it forward acts:

   A | should each be different and performed to three different people.

   B | be performed on our OU campus and/or Athens community.

   C | cannot be monetary.

   D | must be completed prior to delivering your presentation.

   Important: No sources are required for this presentation

2 | Deliver a 3–5 minute informative presentation to your class that narrates your *pay it forward* experiences. Your presentation must follow the *pay it forward* discussion outline included with the assignment description.

3 | Lead a 2–3 minute discussion in which you answer your peers questions and share your reflections on your *pay it forward* acts of kindness.

Outline

For this presentation, use the *Pay it Forward presentation* outline as you prepare this presentation.

- The outline must be written in complete sentences.
- Turn in a copy of your typed Pay It Forward Presentation Outline (one half to one page) to SafeAssign.

Delivery and Notes

You *can* use notecards to deliver this presentation. You should follow the guidelines regarding notecards in your COMS 1030 guidebook (see page 47).

PAY IT FORWARD DISCUSSION OUTLINE EXAMPLE

Introduction

- Attention Getter
- Thesis
- Preview

Transition: Full-sentence transition to body of presentation

Main Point I—Pay It Forward #1

A | Explain the act

B | Why were you compelled to complete this act?

C | What did you learn from this act of kindness?

Transition: Full-sentence transition to second point

Main Point II—Pay It Forward #2

A | Explain the act

B | Why were you compelled to complete this act?

C | What did you learn from this act of kindness?

Transition: Full-sentence transition to third point

Main Point III—Pay It Forward #3

    A | Explain the act

    B | Why were you compelled to complete this act?

    C | What did you learn from this act of kindness?

Transition: Full-sentence transition to conclusion

Conclusion

- Overview
- Re-state thesis
- Memorable closing

INSTRUCTOR EVALUATION OF PAY IT FORWARD SPEECH ASSIGNMENT

Speaker's Name: _____ Total Points: _____ /50

Time Infraction: _____ Time: _____

Use this legend to understand the quality of your performance in each category.

"+" Well Done   "o" Okay/Average   " – " Needs Improvement   "×" Not Included

_____ **Introduction   (6 Points)**

_____ Gained attention
_____ State thesis clearly
_____ Stated preview clearly

_____ **Body   (20 Points)**

_____ Main points clear
_____ Organization effective
_____ Used precise, clear and descriptive
_____ Clear transitions

_____ **Conclusion   (6 Points)**

_____ Restated thesis
_____ Reviewed main points
_____ Made presentation memorable

_____ **Delivery   (8 Points)**

_____ Used vocal variety (pitch, rate, volume)
_____ Used appropriate articulation/pronunciation
_____ Established eye contact with audience
_____ Used appropriate gestures and body movement, facial expressions
_____ Used notecards effectively

_____ **Discussion Facilitation   (10 Points)**

_____ Maintained time requirements (2–3 minutes)
_____ Prompted the audience for questions about their pay it forward experience
_____ Questions were answered fully and ethically
_____ Evidence of time spent preparing for likely questions

Speeches have a 15 second grace period over/under time limit without penalty. Speeches that go 16–29 seconds over/under the time limit will be reduced by 3 points. Speeches that go 30 seconds over/under the time limit will be reduced by 5 points. Excessive time infraction can result in larger penalty per discretion of Instructor.

COMS 1030 | 31

Presentational Strengths:

Opportunities for Improvement:

Chapter 5 IMPROMPTU SPEECH ASSIGNMENT

BY MELISSA WELLER

IMPROMPTU SPEECH ASSIGNMENT

ASSIGNMENT RATIONALE

Impromptu Speeches are speaking events students will encounter many times throughout their academic, professional, and personal lives. This assignment provides an opportunity for students to understand that even with little preparation, any speaking event can be effective and interesting.

Time: 2–3 minutes

One notecard allowed

ASSIGNMENT HIGHLIGHTS

ASSIGNMENT'S CONNECTION TO OVERALL COURSE OBJECTIVES

After completing this assignment students will be able to:

- Understand and use the basic elements of nonverbal delivery, keyword notecards, and organizational patterns.
- Apply ethical communication by incorporating the use of language that is adapted to their audience.
- Demonstrate credibility through competence, trustworthiness, and dynamism throughout the presentation.

ASSIGNMENT'S GENERAL LEARNING OBJECTIVES

After completing this assignment, students will be able to:

- Identify information about fellow classmates experiences.
- Create a 2–3 minute, impromptu speech with little preparation.
- Use a topical organizational pattern.
- Use language that effectively captures the audience's attention and engages them throughout the monologue.
- Deliver an impromptu presentation that includes effective and appropriate contact with the audience, gesturing, and movement.
- Deliver an impromptu presentation with minimal vocal disfluencies/vocal pauses and varied intonation and voice inflection.

ASSIGNMENT OVERVIEW AND COMPONENTS

Overview: Students will have three minutes in class to prepare a 2–3 minute impromptu speech that focuses on their futures. The impromptu speech provides an opportunity to practice verbal and nonverbal communication, critically thinking, and building credibility through speech by being genuine in your communication.

Points Available: 25 points.

Impromptu Days: You will have **no advance notice** of when this speech will occur. This simulates the nature of impromptu speaking. Your Instructor may decide that these speeches occur all in one day or over a series of days.

Components:

1 | Students will choose one of several prompts provided by the Instructor. Students will then have three minutes to prepare and write a keyword notecard. The prompt will be something related to your interests.

2 | Students will deliver the impromptu speech in front of the class.

HOW TO PREPARE ON YOUR IMPROMPTU DAY

- Write and submit *one* note card in preparation for this speech.
- Practice eye contact, gesturing, movement, etc.
- Attempt to create a topical organizational pattern that makes sense for their prompt.
- Relax! You are speaking about yourself, no one knows you better than *you*.

*Be sure to have the Student Guidebook with you each day in order to have your Instructor Evaluation Form on the day you give your Impromptu Speech.

INSTRUCTOR EVALUATION OF IMPROMPTU SPEECH ASSIGNMENT

Speaker's Name: _____ Total Points: _____ /25

Topic: _____ Time: _____

Use this legend to understand the quality of your performance in each category.

"+" Well Done   "o" Okay/Average   " – " Needs Improvement   "×" Not Included

_____ **Speech Content   (10 Points)**

    _____ Speaker established credibility
    _____ Speaker was engaging
    _____ Speaker had a clear purpose (thoroughly explained goal of speech)
    _____ The content of the speech was well organized
    _____ The speech included interesting content related to the prompt

_____ **Delivery   (15 Points)**

    _____ Speaker made effective eye contact with the audience
    _____ Speaker used an appropriate speaking pitch/rate/volume
    _____ Speaker used few disfluencies (i.e., um, like, etc.)
    _____ Speaker gestured naturally and appeared at ease
    _____ Speaker used *one* notecard with keywords only

Comments:

Chapter 6

KEEPING IT CLASSY IN COLLEGE: A NO-NONSENSE GUIDE TO ACADEMIC INTEGRITY

BY SONIA IVANCIC

KEEPING IT CLASSY IN COLLEGE: A NO-NONSENSE GUIDE TO ACADEMIC INTEGRITY

PLAGIARISM

Let's face it; plagiarism is not the most exciting topic. When teachers bring up plagiarism in class, they can see student's eyes droop and heads nod in disinterest almost instantly. However, when these students have to meet with their teacher's to discuss plagiarism in their own work, all of a sudden the topic becomes much more important and relevant. These students often feel emotional, confused, stressed, guilty, and/or remorseful. As teachers, it is our intent to minimize the likelihood that you will commit intentional or unintentional plagiarism by providing you with the tools to understand what plagiarism is and how to avoid it. Preventing plagiarism is not just a matter of being a good or honest person; it requires that you maintain academic integrity in your own work. This chapter offers five best practices that should ensure that you do not (even accidentally) commit plagiarism.

WHAT IS PLAGIARISM?

Ohio University considers plagiarism a form of academic misconduct, and defines it as "the presentation of the ideas or the writing of someone else as one's own" (n.d., para. 5). Plagiarism is a problem because you are taking credit for the ideas or the phrasing of someone else. It is acceptable to use other people's ideas, but you must make sure you indicate this through in-text citations (see Jama & Ross, Chapter 13: APA Guidelines). Part of earning a college degree is being able to proficiently complete assignments on your own. This is why colleges and universities, like OU, have an interest in whether you are doing your own work. Furthermore, it is important that Ohio University maintains rigorous standards for academic integrity because these standards help make your degree respectable and distinguished. The community standards website (Ohio University, n.d.) explains that if a university has low standards about plagiarism or cheating a degree from that school becomes less valuable. In reality, when someone engages in plagiarism it effects the entire OU family-past, present, and future.

Not only do universities want to make sure their students are proficiently completing their degrees, these universities are a part of a community of scholars. Since attending OU, you might have noticed that universities have values and cultural practices that differ from what you experienced in high school. One of these values is that other people's writing and research is taken very seriously (Parsons, 2015). A philosophy professor at the University of Houston Clear-Lake explained that "For an academic, there is something sacred about a citation. The proper citation of a source is a small tribute to the hard work, diligence, intelligence and integrity of someone dedicated enough to make a contribution to knowledge" (Parsons, 2015, para. 9). In order to succeed in the university community, you are expected to contribute to knowledge and to properly cite others who have done the same.

Ohio University expects that students uphold honesty and integrity in their work. In order to do this, students must first understand what honesty and integrity look like from a scholarly standpoint. Now let's discuss the similarities and differences between intentional and unintentional plagiarism.

INTENTIONAL PLAGIARISM

Plagiarism can take many different shapes, and maintaining academic integrity means avoiding all forms of plagiarism. In the most obvious cases, students will turn in other people's work, or parts of other people's work, with their name on it—this is considered intentional plagiarism. Other examples of intentional plagiarism include turning in an entire paper you did not write, paragraphs from a friend's speech outline, copying and pasting from the Internet without providing a citation. These instances of plagiarism are easy for most students to identify and understand, and in most all of these cases, it is evident that the student who plagiarized should have known that what they did was dishonest and intentional.

UNINTENTIONAL PLAGIARISM

You may be surprised to find that students also commit plagiarism *on accident*. Researchers' call this unintentional plagiarism (DeLong, 2012). Plagiarism is still considered plagiarism regardless of whether it was intentional or accidental. Below, we will explore examples like this of plagiarism that are not so obvious.

In one example, a student with the pseudonym "Eli," edited a peer's paper during a class peer-review. When Eli turned in a final copy of his paper it was very similar to the one that he peer-reviewed. In this instance, Eli did not directly copy any of his peer's sentences. You may not think this is plagiarism, because the student used his own words and all of the phrasing was original. However, this example *is considered plagiarism*. The ideas, main claims, and organizational structure that Eli used were so close to that of his peer's rough draft that Eli could not claim that the ideas were his own. Eli said that his intention was not to plagiarize, but he acknowledged that he was trying to use some of the ideas from his peer's paper to improve his own paper. This is an instance of a student who plagiarized, but not intentionally.

In this second example, we will look at an excerpt from a hypothetical informative speech outline on ADHD (attention deficit/hyperactivity disorder).

> *Here is the excerpt from the student's outline:*

> A study suggests that for children with attention disorders, hyperactive movements mean better performance on tasks that require concentration (Kamenetz, 2015).

> *Here is the excerpt from the article they cited:*

> "A new study suggests that for children with attention disorders, hyperactive movements meant better performance on a task that requires concentration" (Kamenetz, 2015, para. 2).

The question is, do you think is this considered plagiarism? Yes, it is. Although the student cited the source, they used an indirect citation, which indicates only that the ideas were the author's. In this case, the student is presenting the writing as her own, when it actually is someone else's. The student needs to put this information in her own words to avoid plagiarism. In cases where students plagiarize by not paraphrasing correctly, many of them plagiarized unintentionally. Below is an example of how you could rephrase the original source's writing to avoid plagiarism.

> *Appropriate paraphrasing:*

> Although people typically consider hyperactive movements distracting, evidence from a 2015 research study found that children with ADHD have better concentration and perform better on tasks when they are able to move around (Kamenetz, 2015).

Notice in the above example that the phrasing, sentence structure, and word choice have changed significantly. This is what you should strive for in your speeches—use the ideas from your sources but make the words your own and make sure you cite the source to give them credit. Although this second example is hypothetical, it reflects one of the most common instances of plagiarism COMS 1030 instructors see in speech outlines. It is worth your time to take the time and care to paraphrase appropriately. Even if you plagiarize on accident (or intentionally), you are still committing plagiarism–and there are potential consequences.

CONSEQUENCES FOR PLAGIARISM

At Ohio University, the consequences for plagiarism can vary. Your Instructor or professor will take into account the specific instance of plagiarism, the assignment, overall course expectations, and University policy when deciding how to handle an instance of plagiarism. Your COMS 1030 Instructor will first have a conversation with you in consultation with the COMS 1030 Course Director. Consequences can include a failing grade on the assignment, a failing grade in the class, and/or a referral to OU's Office of Community Standards and Student Responsibility, where the student will go through disciplinary measures with the University. If the Office of Community Standards and Student Responsibility finds a student responsible for academic misconduct, the student may be expelled, suspended, put on probation, or may receive other school sanctions deemed appropriate for the infraction (see Ohio University, n.d.).

Below are five best practices for avoiding plagiarism. You can use these tips to avoid the consequences explained above!

FIVE BEST PRACTICES FOR AVOIDING PLAGIARISM

1 | **Never copy or turn in anyone else's work.**

This means that you should never copy or turn in work from your friends, websites on the Internet, or books and claim it as your own. Sometimes students copy the work of others when they find the assignment challenging or when they run out of time to complete the assignment. Start your assignments early enough so that you can ask your Instructor questions. If you run out of time, or have an emergency and cannot complete the assignment, it is always better to communicate the situation to your professor rather than to hand in plagiarized work.

2 | **Never allow other students to submit your work as their own.**

By this point, it is clear that you should not give your work to a friend knowing they are going to copy part or all of it and claim it as their own. But, once you lend your work to someone else, you have no control over what they do with it. Your friend could give your assignment to someone else that you do not even know, and even friends may copy your work if they panic, get frustrated, or have a lapse of conscience. The moral of the story is that you should be careful lending your work to other peers and friends, even if you are just providing them with an example. If someone copies your work, you will also be held responsible. Making sure that others do not copy your own work helps you develop and maintain your own credibility as a student and a peer. You want to protect your credibility with everything you have.

3 | Cite all of your sources correctly.

There are two parts to this. First, fully cite your sources (see Jama & Ross, Chapter 13: APA Guidelines). Every time you use any information from an outside source, be it a book, website, newspaper article, YouTube video, or anything else, you must cite where you received this information. Furthermore, if you are providing information that is not considered general knowledge, you need to cite a source explaining where the information comes from.

Second, we want to emphasize the word *correctly* here. You can cite your sources, but in some cases, if you do not cite the source correctly, you could be committing plagiarism. For example, in COMS 1030 we use the APA citation style. It is important to understand how to use APA to cite someone's ideas (an indirect citation) and to know how to use APA when citing the exact words of others (a direct citation). Think about it: you would never quote Dr. Martin Luther King, Jr. without putting what he said in quotation marks. Use these same standards for anyone else's words. If you are quoting someone you *must* indicate this with a direct citation (quotation marks, last name, date, and page/paragraph number). Using someone's exact words without a correct citation indicates that you are claiming those words as your own creation—when those words are not your creation, this is plagiarism.

4 | Paraphrase correctly: make sure you use your own words.

As mentioned above, students often plagiarize in speech outlines because they do not paraphrase adequately. When you turn in any written assignment, your instructors consider the writing to be *yours*. You did the research, created your thesis, decided on the main arguments to use, and chose the evidence that best supports these claims. This means that when using examples or evidence from another source, you should rephrase it and put the information into your own words. You will still give your sources credit for the ideas (through an indirect citation), but you are indicating that the phrasing is your own. Paraphrasing appropriately can be challenging, but it is an opportunity for you to be creative, and it is an important factor in avoiding plagiarism.

5 | Use plagiarism software detectors to check your own work.

In COMS 1030 we use software (e.g., SafeAssign) for your speech outlines and speech critiques to make sure our students are completing their own work and maintaining academic integrity. This software is designed to compare your work to the work of other students, published materials, or Internet websites, and to indicate instances that 'match' these other sources. Many of your professors in other classes also have you upload your papers, outlines, or homework assignments through software that helps detect plagiarism (such as SafeAssign or Turnitin). Most of the time, when you upload your work, you can also view these reports yourself to make sure that you are not matching the words of your sources too closely. We advise you to use these plagiarism detection programs to your own advantage by checking your work. If something looks problematic, you may have the opportunity to fix it and upload a new copy of the outline before the due date.

CONCLUSION

You are not likely to entertain a crowd or get a date with your advanced knowledge about plagiarism, but having a firm understanding of this topic can help you avoid making mistakes in the future and it may even earn you a job—yes people are paid to know how to avoid lawsuits by correctly citing sources! When conversations about plagiarism and academic integrity come up during class, resist the temptation to let your mind wander. As students, you have the privilege to share your knowledge, stories, perspectives, and insight with others. Following the advice of this guidebook and these five best practices in this Chapter can help you share your ideas in an honest and ethical manner. In the end, this makes you more credible as a communicator.

REFERENCES

DeLong, D. (2012). Propensity toward unintentional plagiarism. *Global Education Journal,* 2012, 136–154.

Kamenetz, A. (2015). Vindication for fidgeters: Movement may help students with ADHD concentrate. *NPR.* Retrieved from http://www.npr.org/sections/ed/2015/05/14/404959284/fidgeting-may-help-concentration-for-students-with-adhd

Parsons, K. M. (2015, May 14). Message to my freshman students. *Huffington Post.* Retrieved from http://www.huffingtonpost.com/keith-m-parsons/message-to-my-freshman-st_b_7275016.html

Ohio University. (n.d.) Information for students: Upholding honesty. Retrieved from http://www.ohio.edu/communitystandards/academic/students.cfm

Chapter 7 OUTLINING

BY TIM MCKENNA*

*Heather J. Carmack, Kevin R. Meyer, Craig M. Pinkerton, Mike Parsons, and Dan West contributed to earlier versions of this chapter.

OUTLINING

Outlining is one of the most useful skills you can learn, one that will benefit you in your writing endeavors far beyond this public speaking class. An outline helps you lay out your ideas by structuring them in a coherent and logical order. Additionally, an outline helps you spot "holes" in your writing and flaws in the arguments you construct. In this class you will need to turn in formal sentence outlines. The purpose of this chapter is to provide you with practical advice to develop the fundamental skills for outlining. Following the guidelines and advice in this chapter should help you to construct a basic outline for the speeches that follow.

USING INVENTION AND ORGANIZATION TO CREATE YOUR OUTLINE

Topic

First things first: choose your topic. Be sure to consider your topic carefully before you get it approved because once you start the outlining process there is little room to go back and change your topic and still be successful in your speech presentation. If you have questions or concerns about your topic, talk to your Instructor to see if they can help you establish the topic as a foundation for the outlining process.

Purpose

With your topic in mind it is essential that you understand the purpose of your speech. You need to know whether your purpose is to inform, to persuade, or to acknowledge a special occasion before you will be able to write your thesis statement and develop your main points. As described in your textbook, each speech has a general and specific purpose. This will vary depending on each of the different speeches in this course, and you need this information to create an effective outline. Look at your speech assignments to discern the general purpose of your speech, and then work with your Instructor to decide what the specific purpose of your speech will be.

Thesis

Now that you have a topic and purpose you are ready to develop your thesis statement for the speech. Your textbook explains what a thesis statement is and gives you several examples. While the particular thesis statement will vary depending on the speech you are writing it is important that it is *one clear declarative sentence that encompasses what will be addressed in your speech.* This is the foundation of your speech so this is something to pay close attention to as if it is too broad or too narrow it may be hard to develop your main points. Take your specific purpose into consideration and then think about the goal you want to portray in your speech. Once you recognize the goal it will be easier to ground your thesis with this in mind.

Body of Your Speech

Now that you know what your speech will be about, it's time to start planning the speech itself. Sometimes people think that you should start at the beginning and write until you get to the end. But actually a much better process is to work on the body of your speech first and save the introduction until later. So, the next step in outlining is to figure out the main points of your speech.

Choose Main Points

There are a few things to think about when developing your main points. The main points should obviously support your thesis statement. The main points also need to conform to the organizational pattern you choose and the specific purpose of your speech. Your main points should be the largest arguments or points that have emerged from your research. Points should be related to each others but not address the same information. Each speech assignment provides you with some guidance on how to choose main points, and you can take a look at the example outlines for each of the speeches as they depict good representations of speeches conducted by former students. All of this information will be explained in the chapter that relates to the specific speech you are working on, but it is essential to remember the outlining process and that main points should not be developed until you have a clear declarative thesis to work from.

Select Subpoints

Once you have your main points you can figure out the subpoints for each of them. Each main point will typically have two or three subpoints, which are pieces of information or evidence that support your main points. These points form the body of your speech and need to conform to the particular requirements of your speech assignment. Your Instructor can help your choose appropriate subpoints to best meet the specific purpose of your speech.

Introduction

Now that you have an outline of the body of your speech, you are ready to write the introduction. The introduction is one of the most important parts of any speech. Whether you are speaking to your classmates or giving a public address to thousands of people, your introduction gives your audience many reasons why they should listen to you. There are several parts of an introduction that help you gain your audience's attention. These include: *Attention Getter, Audience Relevance, Speaker Credibility, Thesis Statement,* and *Preview Statement.* Although this may sound like a lengthy beginning to your speech it is the basic structure you will use for most of the speeches in this course.

Attention Getter

This is the first part in the introduction and the purpose is to captivate and grab your audience's attention. There are several methods you can use to accomplish this which are explained further in your textbook, but one important aspect to think about is your audience. First choose an attention getter that you think is most appropriate for the topic, and then adapt the specifics of that method to your audience.

Audience Relevance

After you have grabbed your audience's attention, the next goal is to keep their attention and this is where audience relevance comes into play. For this, you need to think about the audience you are speaking to and ask yourself a few questions: Why should they care about what I am talking about? How can they relate to this topic? Why is it important for them to listen? If you can answer at least one of these questions in this section you will be providing your audience with yet another reason to keep listening.

Speaker Credibility

After you have explained why the audience should listen to your speech, it is essential to explain why you are qualified to speak on this topic. Once again ask yourself a few questions: Why am I speaking on this topic? What is my background in relation to this topic? Why should people listen to me speak about this topic? If you can begin answering these questions you will be able to showcase why you are a credible speaker that the audience should continue listening to.

Thesis Statement

Now that the audience is sitting up in their seats and interested in what you have to say it is important that you tell them what you are going to be talking about. You should clearly state the thesis of your speech. This is the essence of your speech so it is important to emphasize it in your introduction. If the audience does not understand your thesis it will be hard for them to follow the direction of your speech, and your speech will not be very effective.

Preview Statement

Finally, you have come to the closing statement of your introduction. In the preview you will briefly explain the main points of your speech. The preview statement should list the points in the same order they will appear in your speech. This helps your audience understand not only the direction of your speech but also what to look forward to as they now have a glimpse into the essence of the speech.

Conclusion

Finally, you are ready to write your conclusion. While the introduction grabs the audience's attention, the conclusion wraps up the speech and gives the audience a key takeaway message. Just like introductions there are several important components of the conclusion that need to be addressed in order to make your speech successful. These include: *Review of Main Points, Restate Thesis,* and *Decisive Closing.* While these may sound redundant it is your goal to remind your audience of the importance of your speech without plainly repeating what was just said.

Review of Main Points

If you look back to your introduction you will notice that this part of the conclusion is similar to your preview statement. However, what is important is that it is not an exact restatement of your preview statement because the goal of this part of conclusion is not to introduce the main points, but to wrap-up the main points. Thus, for this part it is important to briefly summarize what was gained through each of the main points. This does not need to be longer than one sentence, but should remind the audience of what was covered.

Restate Thesis

Once again another part of the conclusion that is similar to the introduction. However, the difference in restating the thesis in the conclusion is that you have explained and supported what you are declaring. Thus, when restating the thesis in the conclusion you should demonstrate the salience of your thesis based on the content of your speech.

Decisive Closing

The last thing you want to do before you leave the stage is to give your audience a decisive ending that they will remember. This could involve returning to a story that you started in your introduction, or providing more information on a statistic you provided. The goal of this part of conclusion is to close your speech with something that your audience will remember so they leave the room still thinking about the speech.

Basic Transitions

You are now almost done with your outline. The last thing is to create transitions that guide your audience through your speech. Clear and effective transitions are important so that the audience can follow the organization of your speech without getting confused. Transitions tie together your introduction, body, and conclusion. They also help show connections between your main points. Your transitions should be simple statements that use the language of your main points to explain which point is next. For example, simple transitions include statements like "the first reason I believe ...," and "another reason ...I argue..."

Transitions should be written out completely in your outline and said aloud when delivering the speech. These transitions help provide structure for not only you, but for your audience to follow along as you develop and support your main points. Although transitions might seem like something simple, they are often what determines a well-organized speech versus an unorganized speech.

WRITING OUT YOUR FORMAL SENTENCE OUTLINE

For all of the speeches in this class you will need to create formal sentence outlines. The development of your argument is given logical form and order through the construction of your outline. You have likely had previous classes where instructors required outlines, but those requirements may have asked you to follow a slightly different format. In this course, we require a very specific format that all students must follow. Thus, you will want to pay close attention to the specific directions that follow. A formal sentence outline, as described in your textbook, is similar to the script of a play. All of the ideas in your speech should appear in the formal sentence outline, which acts as a tool to help you develop a stronger, better, and more structured speech. Instructors emphasize formal sentence outlines because they ensure that your central idea and main points are focused, presented in a logical order, and backed with adequate support or evidence.

Additionally, a formal sentence outline is a way to make sure you have all the required parts of a speech, such as transition statements, an adequate introduction, and conclusion. While reviewing your formal sentence outline, you can detect flaws in your speech. The outline helps you fix these flaws and develop a better-structured speech.

When constructing your formal sentence outline, be sure to:

1 | Use a consistent numbering and symbol scheme.

The body of your speech will typically develop 2 or 3 main points or claims. Main points are the key ideas of your speech. Designate these main points with Roman numerals (I, II, and III). Develop each main point with at least 2 subpoints that provide the reasons for the main point or claim you are making. Designate the subpoints with capital letters (A, B, and C). The principle of division states that if a point is divided it must result in at least 2 parts. So, each subpoint that is divided will have at least 2 sub-subpoints, which provide support, examples, or explanation for the subpoint. Designate the sub-subpoints with Arabic numerals (1, 2, and 3). See the sample outlines at the end of each speech assignment for an example of how your outline should look.

2 | Use proper indentation and margins to indicate subordination of ideas.

Always state your main points first and then reinforce, develop, and strengthen them by providing subpoints and sub-subpoints. Some people find it easier to type in the outline structure rather than allowing word processing software to outline for you automatically. As soon as you open Word, go to the "Format" tab at the top of the document. Next open "Bullets and Numbering" and select "None" to turn off the automatic outlining. See the sample outline format below to see what indentation should look like in your outlines.

3 | Use only one idea in each point of your outline.

Each item (main point, subpoint, or sub-subpoint) should convey only a single thought or idea. Clarity is a vital component of effective speaking, so restrict yourself to one idea per item. Overloading too many ideas into a single line of an outline structure can be confusing. Remember, audience members cannot go back to what you said if they did not understand the first time around.

4 | Fulfill other requirements.

You will submit a formal sentence outline when you speak. This outline should be written using full sentences—not single words, phrases, or sentence fragments. Remember that full sentences end with a period, question mark, or exclamation point. Writing in full sentences helps you articulate your ideas and figure out the best wording for your speech.

Also, the 5 parts of your introduction and the 3 parts of your conclusion should be clearly labeled, as indicated on the example outline shown in each speech assignment chapter. It is also helpful if you use brackets or parentheses to indicate things you will do while speaking—for example, gestures you want to use, times you want to move a few steps to help the audience visualize your outline, times you want to change your visual aid(s), or places you want to make dramatic pauses for effect.

SAMPLE OUTLINE FORMAT

All of the above information should help you understand how to organize your outline. When you create your outline, you should format it according to this basic template. Each of your speech assignments provides a sample outline, written by an Ohio University student, and these can also serve as excellent examples for your work.

Introduction

I. Attention Getting

II. Audience Relevance

III. Speaker Credibility

IV. Thesis

V. Preview of Main Points

Transition

Body

I. First Main Point

    A. Subpoint

    B. Subpoint

Transition

II. Second Main Point

    A. Subpoint

    B. Subpoint

Transition

III. Third Main Point

    A. Subpoint

    B. Subpoint

Transition

Conclusion

I.   Review Main Points

II. Restate Thesis

III. Decisive Close

FROM OUTLINE TO NOTECARDS

You will submit your formal sentence outline via SafeAssign prior to your presentation day, and you will not actually speak from the outline. The remaining speeches in this course all use extemporaneous delivery. Therefore, you need to condense your outline onto speaking notecards that you will be able to refer to during your speech. It is helpful to keep in mind a couple of tips when you write your speaking notecard.

First, remember that the objective of extemporaneous speaking is a conversational style of delivery. Accordingly, the notecards you use to speak from should not be a script or duplication of your formal sentence outline. You should not read your speech like a manuscript. Second you must rehearse your speech before your class presentation. This does not mean that you memorize your speech, but you should practice until you can easily recall the main points you want to deliver.

Use your speaking notecards as a reminder of your key points. Include phrases, important words, quotations, statistics, and references that are essential to your speech but may be harder to remember. You will find it helpful to list, in order, the main points and subpoints of your speech in shorthand, using just 1–3 words per point, so you can follow the planned structure and not *skip* important points. Think of your notecards as a *key word outline*. Please notice that the notecards should be limited to 20–30 words (ask your Instructor for specific guidelines) aside from the thesis statement and citations. If there is a difficult or unfamiliar term that you may stumble on while pronouncing, you could spell out the word phonetically to avoid mispronouncing it. Be sure not to write too small on your notecards, or you may have difficulty spotting the information during your speech.

For the speeches you will be delivering in your public speaking class, we believe you should be able to prepare adequate speaking notes using 3×5-inch white index cards.

The following example demonstrates what might be on a notecard.

```
AGD – Hendrix Quotation
ARL—Everyone ♥'s Music
CS— Music is Important
Thesis— Music on the radio should not be censored.
Preview
Transition
MP1— Censorship ↓ F.O.S.
        A. Musicians = free expression
        B. FCC revoke license
Transition
MP2—Censorship = Message Lost
        A. Eminem ex.
        B. "My Fault" explanation
Transition
MP3—Economic Effects
        A. Music Production = Expensive
        B. 2 Albums = $
Transition
Review Main Points
Restate Thesis— Music on the radio should not be censored.
Closing—Support Music
```

Chapter 8 OUT-OF-CLASS SPEECH CRITIQUE ASSIGNMENT

BY DR. ANGELA M. HOSEK*

*Jocelyn M. DeGroot, Ephraim N. Kotey, Laura Russell, and
Jessica Furgerson contributed to earlier versions of this chapter.

OUT-OF-CLASS | SPEECH CRITIQUE ASSIGNMENT

EVALUATING SPEECHES

The goal of this assignment is to provide you with an opportunity to critically analyze and apply the concepts, theories, skills, and ideas you are learning in COMS 1030 to a presentational speaking event within the community.

> Look for the #OCCrit hashtag for speaking events on Twitter!
>
> **COMS 1030 IS ON TWITTER!**
> **@COMS1030_OU**

ASSIGNMENT GUIDELINES

Overview

This assignment has two components. *First*, you will *physically* attend a formal type presentational speaking event outside of class. Viewing online/mediated speaking events is not permissible for this assignment; you must **attend the speaking event in person.** *Second*, you will write a three page critical analysis of the speaking event. This assignment is worth **50 points** of your final course grade.

Written Assignment Criteria

Content

In this paper you have three objectives.

1 | Describe the nature of the event, speaker, and audience.

2 | Select at least *three* aspects of the speaking event that you found most meaningful and strongly connected to our course content.

   Define, justify, and critique **each of the three aspects** you selected using evidence from our course text. In other words, at a minimum you need to cite the course textbook as your form of evidence. Below is a list, although not comprehensive, that you *may* use to guide your critique.

Optional Guiding Questions/Ideas

- How did the speaker gain audience attention? Was it effective?
- How did the speaker make his or her topic relevant to the audience?
- How did the speaker establish his or her credibility?
- Describe and analyze the purpose of the speech.
- Describe the types of support (e.g., statistics, testimony, stories, examples) used by the speaker. How, if at all, were they effective?

- Analyze the speaker's verbal and nonverbal delivery.
- Describe the speaker's use of language. Include such details as word choice, articulation, pronunciation, clarity, vividness, and appropriateness.
- What was your overall reaction to the speech?
- What was the audience's reaction?
- How, if at all, did this experience improve your personal presentational speaking skills?

3 | Describe the meaningfulness of this experience as it relates to your own public speaking knowledge and skill development. In other words, what will you do similarly and/or differently in your future presentations based on this experience?

Citing Sources

The only required published source is your textbook. However, you are encouraged to use additional and relevant published sources, as needed, to support your claims. Citations (in-text and for your reference list) must conform to the guidelines of the most recent edition of the APA Publication Manual (see APA examples in Chapter 13: APA Guidelines).

Format Guidelines

- ☐ 3 pages of content (excluding bibliography)
- ☐ Double-spaced
- ☐ Times New Roman 12-pt font
- ☐ Include page numbers
- ☐ Sources cited in APA format in the reference list (in order to conserve paper, you can place this at the end of the paper with a heading; it does not need to begin on a new page)
- ☐ Using APA format, cite sources in-text to support your claims
- ☐ Paper must reflect technical proficiency (correct grammar, spelling, punctuation, and organization). Proofread carefully. Please review the policy on writing expectations, which is located in your syllabus.

Assessment

Your work will be evaluated using the *Out-of-Class Speech Critique Instructor Form*. You should review this document so you understand how you will be graded.

Due Date

- This assignment is due via Blackboard on the day/time of your COMS 1030 Final Exam period (see Final Exam Schedule on *ohio.edu*).
- If you do not attend the final exam period to engage in the discussion of this assignment with your classmates, you will receive a zero on this assignment.
- To be clear, you must submit the assignment on time (as stated above) and attend class during your COMS 1030 section's final exam period; otherwise, you will receive a zero on this assignment.

INSTRUCTOR EVALUATION OF OUT-OF-CLASS SPEECH CRITIQUE ASSIGNMENT

Speaker's Name: _____ Total Points: _____ /50

Use this legend to understand the quality of your performance in each category.

"+" Well Done   "o" Okay/Average   " – " Needs Improvement   "×" Not Included

I. Paper

_____ **Thoroughness   (10 points)**

_____ Sections are thoroughly described, developed, and supported

_____ **Understanding of Selected Aspects and Connection to Course Content   (30 points)**

_____ At least three aspects of the speaking event are included and clearly identifiable
_____ Quality of critique (includes quality of examples, application to course material, and overall connection to public speaking principles)
_____ Reflected an integrated understanding of how this experience related to student's personal public speaking knowledge and skill development
_____ Appropriate use of supporting evidence

II. Format and Writing of Paper

_____ **Format and Writing   (10 points)**

_____ Writing is clear, focused, style is consistent, well-organized
_____ Paper is free from grammatical and structural errors
_____ Work met requirements of assignment (length and formatting)
_____ Technical preparation and quality of work, proofreading is evident
_____ APA format followed throughout (in-text citations and reference page)

Comments:

Chapter 9 LISTENING: A VITAL COMMUNICATION SKILL

BY HENGJUN LIN AND MARION MENDY

LISTENING A VITAL COMMUNICATION SKILL

Both actively engaging your audience in your speech and being an effective and ethical listener are important to public speaking. This chapter will provide information and practical tips to encourage your audience to listen and improve your own listening skills.

WHY LISTENING IS IMPORTANT

Let's think about the interactive communication model that you learned in the *COMS 1030 ISPEAK* textbook, Chapter 4. In this communication-oriented age, listening is incredibly important (Wolvin & Coakley, 1991). Research shows that listening is strongly correlated with academic success (Canpolat et al, 2015). In other words, students with the highest grades tend to be the strongest listeners (Bommelje, Houston & Smither, 2003). Importantly to COMS 1030, listening is a crucial skill in the context of public speaking, because it is the channel of receiving messages from the speaker. The feedback loop of interaction in communication processes is to some extent determined not only but how well the source packages the message to be listened to but also by how well you, as a listener, can receive messages from the speaker. For instance, listening is the number one crucial skill for business managers (Bolton, 2005).

Listening skills are fundamental to you in two ways. First, it is important to you, as a speaker, since it is a vital way to collect relevant information and ideas from sources such as radio, television, video websites, conversations, and lectures to use in your speeches. Secondly, listening skills are also crucial to you as an audience member. As an audience member, listening critically and effectively is a way to show respect to the speaker, learn something new from others' speeches, and be able to critically analyze and evaluate the information you hear during a speech. In your public speaking class, you will be listening to far more speeches than you deliver, which provides you with a unique opportunity to develop your listening skills.

LISTENING AND CRITICAL THINKING

Here we introduce four skills to help your listen critically (Lucas, 2009).

1 | **Appreciative Listening**

Listening for pleasure or enjoyment, as when we listen to music, a comedy routine, or an entertaining speech.

2 | **Empathic Listening**

Listening to understand and provide emotional support for the speaker, as when a psychiatrist listens to a patient or when we lend a sympathetic ear to a friend in distress.

3 | **Comprehensive Listening**

Listening to understand the message of a speaker, as when we attend a classroom lecture or listen to directions for finding a friend's house.

4 | Critical Listening

Listening to evaluate a message for purposes of accepting or rejecting it, as when we listening to the sales pitch of a used-car dealer or the campaign speech of a political candidate.

In a public speaking class, we deal primarily with comprehensive listening and critical listening. These two types of listening are what you will use the most often in class when listening to speeches. The next section will provide you with some steps that you can take to improve your skills in comprehensive and critical listening.

HOW TO BECOME A BETTER LISTENER

Before we go into how we can improve our listening skills, first we should know what makes poor listening. Discovering these problems will help you reflect on your specific weaknesses in listening. As you read the list below, think about how often you engage in these behaviors during a given class session.

Behaviors that Result in Poor Listening

1 | Not concentrating.

Although our brain is tremendously efficient at processing information, it does not necessarily make listening easy. On the contrary, we can be easily distracted, which makes us not concentrate enough.

2 | Listening too hard.

Sometimes we try really hard to follow every single word of an important speech, because we assume they are equally important. This can lead to missing the speaker's main points.

3 | Jumping to conclusions.

At times we tend to make a quick conclusion based on the limited information we hear from the speaker. If we are not patient enough, we might misunderstand the core value of the speech.

4 | Focusing on delivery and personal appearance.

Remember the content of the speech is more important to listeners. While it is necessary to also focus on the delivery aspect of the speech, too much focus should not be put on the appearance of the speaker. Rather, you must focus more on the content and the performance of the speaker.

Behaviors to Engage in to Become an Active Listener

1 | Resist distractions.

There are two useful tips for you to resist distractions. First, do not be diverted by appearance or delivery. Someone may dress up nicely and not necessarily have a well-polished speech. Second, use your logical thinking to have a holistic view of the speech. You should hear the speaker out before you make your final judgment about the presentation.

2 | Focus your listening.

Here we introduce three ways for you to stay focused on listening.

A | Catch the main points.

As we know, main points are the important basic structure of a speech. It includes the key information that guides you through the speech. A sharp listener will catch the main points and sketch the general appearance of the speech.

B | Listen for evidence.

You also have to listen for evidence in order to have further evaluation about the quality of the speech's argument.

C | Listen for technique.

Examine the methods that speakers use to deliver an effective speech. You can ask yourself: What does the speaker use as an attention getter? Is the language clear, accurate, vivid, and appropriate? Does the speaker adapt to the audience and the occasion?

Now that you have learn some ways of how to improve your listening, it's time for you to go and practice your listening skills when your classmates present their speeches. You can do it!

REFERENCES

Bommelje, R., Houston, J. M., & Smither, R. (2003). Personality characteristics of effective listeners: A five factor perspective. *International Journal of Listening, 17*(1), 32–46.

Bolton, B. (2005). Your career in today's enterprise. *Information Systems Management, 22*(1), 86.

Canpolat, M., Kuzu, S., Yildirim, B., & Canpolat, S. (2015). Active listening strategies of academically successful university students. *Eurasian Journal of Educational Research (EJER),* (60), 163–180. doi:10.14689/ejer.2015.60.10

Lucas, S. E. (2004). *The Art of Public Speaking 11th Edition.*

Wolvin, A. D., & Coakley, C. G. (1991). A survey of the status of listening training in some Fortune 500 corporations. *Communication Education, 40*(2), 152–164.

Chapter 10

THE POWER OF CONNECTING THROUGH STORYTELLING AND STORY SHARING

BY ZAMZAM JAMA WITH CONTRIBUTIONS
FROM REBEKAH P. CRAWFORD

THE POWER OF CONNECTING THROUGH STORYTELLING AND STORY SHARING

Anthropologist and author John D. Niles (1999) stated it best in his book, *The Poetics and Anthropology of Oral Literature,* when he argued that human beings' ability to tell stories distinguished them from the rest of the animal kingdom. He coined the term *Homo Narran* to depict the unique nature of how storytelling developed as a survival tactic that allowed humans to explain, understand, and predict their environment. Narrative is a way of connecting events that happen through time so that they have a relationship that creates meaning. We as humans have used stories for the purpose of making sense of our realities, documenting our histories, evoking emotional connections with each other, expanding our imagination, and inspiring us to action. While the story may be the product, the interactive process of exchanging defining moments in our lives is called storytelling (Bianco, 2011). In storytelling, the speaker has an audience in mind and as a result the story is often modified to adapt to the listening audience for a specific purpose. For example, if a political speaker is giving a speech in front of a concerned group of environmentalists, the speaker could use storytelling as a strategy to build credibility. So, the speaker might talk about how they came to value environmental rights over that of corporate greed. In this case, we can see that the speaker had a specific purpose in mind and a clear understanding of what values were held by the target audience. The speaker was able to use storytelling as communicative act of building relational connections with the audience by sharing defining movements that shape identity. John Coleman (2012) argued that narratives can be used as a strategic tool to connect with an audience. Story sharing is the practice of "engaging all humans as equally valued participants in an ongoing process of creating and revising both individual stories and broader human stories" (Grobstein, 2007, p. 1). Simply put, story sharing is where both the speaker and the audience co-create a meaning in the space between a narrator's words and the audience's ears.

Why are stories, storytelling, and story sharing important in COMS 1030? As noted earlier, individuals use stories to make sense of their realities and share those realities with given audience members to create an intended effect. In this way, storytelling is a way to invite the listener into your experience. When people hear your stories, they can see the world from your perspective. They can feel what you felt and better understand your intentions. As a result, stories can be effectively used in presentations as a means of building credibility, forming lines of argumentation, building evidence, making emotional appeals, educating audiences on specific topics, or enhancing a topic through entertainment. Think back to a speech you heard recently that left an impression on you. What do you remember? Did the speaker tell a story? Did they show some emotion? It is more likely than not that speaker utilized stories as a strategic tool to connect with an audience, and this is only one way narrative can be used to convey meaning. You are no different; you most likely remember that memorable speech because it had an emotional, moral, or rational impact. Because we think about our life, our day, even our identities as stories, it makes sense that in a presentational sense, audiences and speakers gravitate towards stories as a way of understanding and organizing information to make emotional, moral, and rational decisions. Stories are so familiar to us that they are easy for us to hear, absorb, and remember. Keeping that in mind, remember that a speaker's ability to effectively create and utilize storytelling is the difference between keeping an audience engaged and being memorable versus being disinterested and bored. Therefore, the following chapter is structured to help you reflectively navigate how to effectively use stories when constructing your speeches for your COMS 1030 class. In this chapter, you will learn about how audiences evaluate stories, how culture and identity influence the directionality of your tales, what power storytelling has on changing the minds of audiences, and a few helpful tips to keep in mind.

EVALUATING THE CREDIBILITY OF STORIES

Noting that stories are innately powerful, how do we measure the quality of a story? Communication scholar Walter Fisher (1984) posed this exact question when he created the Narrative Paradigm. Fisher noted that humans use stories to make sense of what happens around them and in doing so help guide their behavior. For example, when we hear an ambulance alarm go by, our brains come up with a story to justify why we heard the alarm in order to decrease anxiety and uncertainty. We tell ourselves that someone must have been extremely hurt in an accident and that is why the ambulance rang the alarm. In reality, we do not know this to be the absolute truth. For all we know, it could have been a test run in which no one was hurt. Nevertheless, as humans we gain a sense of calm and rationality when using stories to help explain the phenomena that happen around us. As such, stories have come to hold so much importance in our cultures, that in some cases they can actually be used as evidence. An example of this is the witness testimonies collected by police officers. These testimonies are narratives told by individuals about what they saw and how they understand what occurred during a crime. In a court of law, these stories are seen as credible forms of evidence. This could make us wonder about how we determine if a story is legitimate and not a lie. Fisher asked this same question, and he determined that in order for a story to be credible or logical three criteria must be fulfilled:

- **Coherence:** The parts of a story must hold together well enough to sound reasonable and probable.
- **Fidelity:** A story must be consistent with what audiences know to be true in their lives.
- **Values:** A story's underling messages and lesson must match with things the teller and audience think are important.

In other words, a story must be seen as reasonable, ring true, and affirm certain values in order for an audience to accept it. Remember, that if the audience perceives that a story fails to meet one of the above criteria, they will begin to question the speaker's intent and credibility. Often times, failure of coherence, fidelity, and matching of values will lead to the audience disengaging and/or rejecting the speaker's message. This could lead to the loss of the speaker's ethos in the eyes of the audience and prevent access to pathos for persuasive purposes. Even the use of logos, the speaker's logic, will be compromised once the audience begins to question the integrity of the speaker's character. It is for all these reasons that is it important to evaluate the coherence, fidelity, and values inherent stories before using them in speeches.

As you think about creating stories to use in your presentations in COMS 1030, remember some stories are fictional parables or metaphors that are retold to make a point. At times, stories can purport to be true but may or may not be. Hence, you want to make sure that you check the credibility of a story before repeating it.

Here are a few more questions to keep in mind when creating a story.

- Is my story likely to have happened?
- Does the story sound realistic or probable?
- Do I come across as truthful?
- Am I consistent throughout my story?
- What are the underlying arguments put forward by the story?
- What are the values or world-view framed in the story?
- What do my audiences hold of value?

INFLUENCE OF SELF AND CULTURE

Stories help shape how we come to understand the world. In this way, the audience comes to understand a speaker's worldview and identity, in part, by their choice of words, actions, illustrations, and arguments used in a story. A speaker's identity is often socially constructed; in other words, it is based on their interactions with their given communities and cultures. Cultures influence how individuals see themselves in relation to others and dictate what is considered as appropriate or inappropriate through the development of societal values. This means that no story is innocent. In other words, no story is absent of culture because all stories forward certain cultural values and knowledge claims that cannot be separated from the identity of the speaker. One advantage to this is that stories can be used to connect communities and promote "social cohesion" (Marshall, 2009). We use stories to learn from each other's experiences.

Here are a few questions to help you considers how identity affects the construction of stories.

- What is my identity?
- How do my social identities (i.e., gender identity, race, socio-economic status) shape how I tell the story?
- What are the cultural values that are implied or apparent in my story? (i.e., justice, equality, gender roles, expectations of behavior, etc.)
- How does my culture and identity enhance my story?
- How does my culture and identity inhibit (limit) my story?

POWER AND STORYTELLING

Stories have power! They have the ability to testify against wrong doings and as a result spur social movements. A great example of this is the "I Have a Dream" speech by Dr. Martin Luther King, Jr. that told a story of a world where social injustice based on race did not exist and where people were judged by the merit of their character. As you know, Dr. King's story is commonly invoked to illustrate how stories have the power to persuade and captivate audiences into taking action against injustices. Just as culture is prevalent in stories, so are power systems. Stories have the ability to give voice to the voiceless, and they can be also used to silence voices. Feminist and author Chimamanda Ngozi Adichie (2009) argues this more clearly when she says that "stories matter, stories have been used to dispossess and malign, but stories can also be used to empower and humanize. Stories can break the dignity of a people but stories can also repair that broken dignity" (17:35). It's very important before you incorporate a story into your speech or presentation to consider whose story is being told and whose is being silenced. Civically responsible speakers consider both the intended and unintended consequence of the stories they tell.

Here are a few questions to help you considers how power affects the construction of stories.

- Whose voice is being heard?
- Whose perspective is being silenced?
- What position of privilege do you hold?
- What position of oppression is imposed on you?
- What does your story say about those who are not in position of privilege?
- What does your story say about those who are in position of power?
- What cultural values are upheld or rejected?
- Are you speaking for yourself or speaking for others?

STORYTELLING AND PRESENTING TIPS

Here are a few tips and questions to keep in mind as you use stories to enhance your presentations.

1 | Great storytelling has a purpose.

    A | What is the purpose of your story?

    B | Is the purpose to inform, persuade, or entertain?

    C | What is your intended goal or objective?

    D | What do you want the audience to do with the story?

2 | The best Stories are those from personal experience.

    A | How can you make the story more personable?

    B | How can you use your personal experience and identity to enhance the story?

3 | Draw your audience into the story and into your speech.

    A | What can you do to capture and maintain the audience attention?

    B | How can you utilize imagery, language, and description to decorate a story?

    C | How can you use a story to draw your audience into the topic of your speech?

4 | Have closure in your stories.

    A | How can you end a story in a meaningful way?

    B | How can you make the story memorable?

    C | How can you make your story relatable?

5 | Delivery is just as important as content.

    A | What can you do vocally to enhance the story? (e.g., volume, pitch, rate, tone, pauses, etc.)

    B | What can you do kinetically to enhance the story? (e.g., movements, gestures, posture, eye contact, facial expressions, etc.)

    C | How can you use proxemics to enhance the story? (e.g., moving across the room, use the space and objects around you, etc.)

    D | What can you do chronemically to enhance the story? (e.g., when you tell it and how much you tell throughout your speech.)

    E | How can you use haptics to enhance the story? (e.g., touching, where to touch, how long, etc.)

    F | How can you use appearance and artifacts to enhance the story? (e.g., what you wear, props, objects, etc.)

    G | How often have you practiced telling your story? Who has listened to it and given you feedback on it?

6 | You need all the elements of a story.

  A | What is the theme of your story?

  B | What is the plot of your story?

  C | Who are the characters? Why are they important?

  D | What is the setting?

  E | How will you structure the story?

  F | What is the tone of the story?

7 | Location, Location, Location.

  A | Where you tell your story during a presentation is also important! Consider the advantages and limitations of telling your story in the following locations:

    i | Attention Getter

    ii | Credibility Statement

    iii | Supporting Material for Body Points.

    iv | Transitions Statements

    v | Memorable Closing

8 | Analyze how power, culture, and identity frame your stories and how this could influence the audience.

EXTRA RESOURCE

Need help with where to start and how to structure a story? Utilize the following link on the Eight Classic Storytelling Techniques: http://www.sparkol.com/engage/8-classic-storytelling-techniques-for-engaging-presentations/

REFERENCES

Adichie, C. N. [TEDTalks]. (2009). The danger of a single story. [Video file]. Retrieved from, https://www.youtube.com/watch?v=D9Ihs241zeg

Bianco, J. (2011). Narrative empowerment and the talking cure. *Health Communication, 26,* 297–301.

Coleman, J. (2012). Why collaborative storytelling is the future of marketing. Retrieved from, http://www.fastcompany.com/1826645/why-collaborative-storytelling-future-marketing

Fisher, Walter R. (1985). "The Narrative Paradigm: An Elaboration." in *Communication Monographs 52.* December. pp. 347–367.

Grobstein, P. (2007). Mind, brain, and culture: Story telling and story sharing. Retrieved from, http://serendip.brynmawr.edu/exchange/node/576.

Marshall, L. B. (2009). Everyday storytelling. Retrieved from, http://www.quickanddirtytips.com/business-career/public-speaking/everyday-storytelling.

Niles, J. D. (1999). *Homo Narrans: The poetics and anthropology of oral literature.* Philadelphia: University of Pennsylvania Press.

Chapter 11 INFORMATIVE SPEECH ASSIGNMENT

BY JESSICA FURGERSON*

*Heather J. Carmack, Kevin R. Meyer and Craig M. Pinkerton contributed to previous versions of this chapter.

INFORMATIVE SPEECH ASSIGNMENT

In this assignment you will craft an informative speech. As you craft your informative speech, remember to follow the steps you have learned for writing effective outlines. This chapter expands those ideas by describing how they fit with the informative speech assignment.

> General Purpose: To Inform
>
> Time: 5–6 minutes
>
> Requires research—Minimum of 5 appropriate sources
>
> One to three notecards allowed
>
> **ASSIGNMENT HIGHLIGHTS**

SELECTING A TOPIC AND PURPOSE

After doing some brainstorming about potential topics, it is time to select one for your speech. Remember—an informative presentation should increase your audience's knowledge of a particular topic or teach them something new (e.g., a cheaper way to recycle paper). It should NOT ask them to change their attitudes, actions or beliefs (e.g., telling them "you should recycle"). If your topic does that, save it for the persuasive speech later this term.

As you review your topic, keep the following ideas in mind: you must be able to *relate the presenter to the topic* as well as *relate the topic to the audience*. Relating the presenter to the topic means you should choose something that you know about or that interests you. Some ideas might include highlighting the traditions, foods, or important places of a city that you enjoy such as New York or Chicago; describing an activity that you are involved in like rugby or scuba diving; or discussing something about sustainability that you are interested in like local food, sustainable farming, or different models for alternative energy. With the informative speech, you become the class expert on your topic. Additionally, you need to think about how to relate the topic to your audience. One way to help narrow your list of topics is to ask yourself, "So what? Why would my audience want or need to care about this particular idea, place or activity?" If it doesn't seem like your audience has any common interest in your topic, or the only thing you can come up with is that it might apply to college students in general, you may want to think about choosing something else.

Specific purpose statements and thesis statements help clarify your topic and the purpose of your speech. For the informative speech, your specific purpose statement will aim at informing the audience of your topic. It should include an observable goal for what you want your audience to take away from the speech. The thesis statement is a more catchy and memorable version of the specific purpose statement. It should be written as one complete and declarative sentence so your topic is clear to your audience. For example:

Topic Area: Climate change

General Purpose: To inform

Specific Purpose: My audience will be able to explain the controversies around global climate change.

Poor Thesis Statement: You should know more about climate change.

Good Thesis Statement: Our global climate is changing, but there is controversy about both the causes and effects.

ORGANIZATIONAL SPEECH PATTERNS

Next, you need to choose how to organize your information. The informative and persuasive speeches can follow several different organizational patterns. It is up to you to choose the best pattern for your speech. Your textbook discusses several different options for organizing your informative speech, and your outline should utilize one of the following organizational patterns.

1 | The *time-sequence pattern* describes the order of events or steps as they actually would or have occurred. You may want to consider this format for biographical or historical speeches, such as the development of the Space Program.

Topic Area: The history of the U.S. Space Program

General Purpose: To inform

Specific Purpose: My audience will be able to explain the development of the U.S. Space Program.

Thesis Statement: The development of the U.S. Space Program was a pivotal event of the 20th century.

Main Points:
    I.   NASA was first created in 1958 by President Dwight Eisenhower.

    II.   The next major step for the U.S. Space Program was the development of the manned space flight program in 1961.

    III.   The biggest achievement for the U.S. Space Program came in 1969 when NASA astronauts successfully landed on the moon.

2 | The *spatial pattern* demonstrates how items are related in space. This may be helpful if your speech is explaining how a farmer's market is set up, or where some of the key landmarks are in an important area. Here's a sample main-point outline using the spatial pattern:

Topic Area: Venice, Italy

General Purpose: To inform

Specific Purpose: My audience will be able to describe some of the famous sites and landmarks in Venice, Italy.

Thesis Statement: Venice is home to numerous famous landmarks.

Main Points:
    I.   The first site I recommend visiting in Venice is Saint Mark's Basilica.

    II.   From Saint Mark's, you should walk over to visit Rialto Bridge.

    III.   Finally, no trip to Venice is complete without seeing the Grand Canal.

3 | The *topical pattern* breaks down a large topic into smaller sub-topics. Keep in mind that the points should be related to each other. For example, you could use this pattern to describe three ways the Athens area promotes sustainability. Here's a sample main-point outline using the topical pattern:

Topic Area: Sustainability in Southeastern Ohio

General Purpose: To inform

Specific Purpose: My audience will be able to explain how organizations in Athens promote sustainability.

Thesis Statement: There are many efforts to promote economic and environmental sustainability in the Athens area.

Main Points:
    I.   The Athens Farmer's Market gives local farmers and merchants a chance to sell their products directly to local consumers.

    II. Several local restaurants advocate the idea of a "30-Mile Meal."

    III. Ohio University's Office of Sustainability partners with local organizations to host educational events for community members and students.

4 | The *cause-effect pattern* describes why something occurs, usually tracing an effect back to the cause, or vice versa. Notice that the cause-effect pattern only has two main points, not three. Because of this, it's important to be sure to have several subpoints for both the cause and effect—more than you would probably use in other organizational patterns. Here's a sample main-point outline using the cause-effect pattern:

Topic Area: Skin Cancer

General Purpose: To inform

Specific Purpose: My audience will be able to identify the causes and effects of skin cancer.

Thesis Statement: Skin cancer has several causes and many effects.

Main Points:
    I.   Skin cancer is primarily caused by exposure to the sun's ultraviolet light.

    II. Too much sun exposure can lead to changes in your skin, including cancer.

SAMPLE

FORMAL SENTENCE OUTLINE (INFORMATIVE)

INFORMATIVE SPEECH OUTLINE: COMS 1030

Title of Speech: Understanding Alzheimer's

Specific Purpose: My audience will understand the causes, symptoms, and treatments for Alzheimer's disease.

Thesis: As one of the top leading causes of death in the United States, Alzheimer's Disease emotionally and physically affects patients and their families.

Introduction

I. Attention Getter

Picture your life throughout the next 40 years. What happened? Did your boyfriend finally pop the question? Was your child healthy? Did you get your dream job? Did she say the big "I do?" Imagine all the milestones that you'll be going through. Image all the moments that make your heart skip a beat, the happiness that moves you to tears, and the endless nights with your best friends. Now imagine slowly forgetting everything and everyone you've ever known and experienced. Imagine being unable to do simple tasks without assistance. Imagine not knowing the love of your life.

II. Audience Relevance Link

According to The National Institutes of Health, this, unfortunately, is a reality for 5.1 million people. The fatal disease attacks 1 in 8 older Americans every year, slowly depriving them of what they spent the last 60 years building up and collecting.

III. Credibility

When I was 13, my grandma lost her battle with Alzheimer's Disease. Four years after her diagnosis, she began to confuse me with my brother. That's when I knew something was really wrong. I never imagined that two years later, I would be sitting by her bed praying that she would speak or at least acknowledge one of us.

IV. Thesis

As one of the top leading causes of death in the United States, Alzheimer's Disease emotionally and physically affects the patient and their families.

V. Preview

Today, I will discuss the causes, symptoms, and help offered for Alzheimer's Disease.

Transition: First we will discuss what causes Alzheimer's.

Body

I. Although the main and direct cause of Alzheimer's Disease is unknown, doctors have found many common factors among patients (Park, 2010).

    A. Genetics is the most common factor that is seen ("What is Alzheimers," 2009). On my mom's side of the family, all females have passed away from Alzheimer's, my grandma being the first of her sisters. Assuming that this on-going trend continues, my mom and I will both eventually have it.

    B. Through brain scans, doctors have pointed out plaques and tangles within the brain caused by aluminum. These affect cell communication and transportation, which leads to the brain cells dying off.

    C. Most patients are around 65 years old, so age also plays a role (National Institute on Aging, 2011).

    D. Even though my grandma was the youngest out of her siblings, she smoked cigarettes, which doctors believe to be a trigger for earlier development of the disease.

    E. Some other common factors seen among patients are head injuries, Down's syndrome, excess of the protein ABeta in the brain, and being of the female gender.

Transition: Without a definite known cause, doctors must rely on symptoms to detect this tragedy.

II. The American Health Assistance Foundation breaks the symptoms associated with Alzheimer's down into three stages.

    A. Stage one lasts 2–4 years and is tricky to catch. Since Alzheimer's affects the elderly, symptoms of stage one are often mistaken for simply the downsides of aging. Minor memory failures, being withdrawn for social events, having poor judgment, and getting lost more often are all on the list for stage one symptoms (Alzheimer's Association, n.d.).

    B. Lasting anywhere from 2–10 years, stage two is the longest of the three stages. Symptoms of stage two become significantly more visible than those in stage one. These symptoms include being disabled, needing assistance with more complicated daily tasks, more serious memory loss, confusion, and irritability.

    C. Towards the end of the long battle with Alzheimer's, stage three hits, lasting only 1–3 years. At this point, there is very little a patient can do. Eating, talking, swallowing, and controlling their own bladder become near impossible without assistance. Memory becomes basically nonexistent and the body continues to shut down. Constant care is needed at this point either at home or in a care center (Med Net, n.d.).

Transition: Even though Alzheimer's is without a cure, there are things that can help prolong the onset of stage three.

III. There is currently no known way to prevent or cure Alzheimer's disease, but researchers are working towards one every day.

    A. They are testing out new drugs, forms of medications, and looking over the factors that seem to be common in patients. There are medications out there though to help the process along (Glass, 2009).

B. Medications are available to help lessen memory loss, take some of the steam from the emotional mood swings, and maintain a sleep cycle (Crook, 1986).

C. It's also important to keep a normal, routine life.

Transition: Alzheimer's Disease affects millions of people and their families every year. While the patient suffers, the families must sit by and watch their loved one slowly slip away from them and there is nothing they can do about it.

Conclusion

I. Review Main Points

I've had first hand experience as I watched my grandma go through the stages while medications began to no longer be an option. The disease has unknown causes and zero cures.

II. Restate Thesis

Alzheimer's Disease emotionally and physically affects the patient and their families as it continues to be one of the leading causes of death.

III. Decisive Closing

Hopefully someday, scientists and researchers will finally find a way to stop this tragedy. Thank you.

References

Alzheimer's Association. (n.d.). *Ten Signs of Alzheimer's.* Retrieved from http://www.alz.org/alzheimers_ disease_10_signs_of_alzheimers.asp

Crook, T. (1986). *Treatment development strategies for Alzheimer's disease.* Madison, CT: Mark Powley Press.

Glass, J. (2009, June 16). Research in Alzheimer's Disease. *Alzheimer's Disease Health Center.* Retrieved from http://www.webmd.com/alzheimers/guide/alzheimers-research

Mayo Clinic. (2011, January 18). *Alzheimer's Disease: Causes.* Retrieved from http://www.mayoclinic.com/health/ alzheimersdisease/DS00161/DSECTION=causes

Med Net (n.d.). *Alzheimer's Disease Causes, Stages, and Symptoms.* Retrieved from http://www.medicinenet.com/ alzheimers_disease_causes_stages_and_symptoms/article.htm

National Institute on Aging. (July 2011). *Alzheimer's Disease Fact Sheet.* Retrieved from http://www.nia.nih.gov/ alzheimers/publication/alzheimers-disease-fact-sheet

Park, A. (2010, October 25). Alzheimer's Unlocked. *Time,* 176, 53–59.

What Is Alzheimer's Disease? What Causes Alzheimer's Disease? (2009, July 31). *Health News.* Retrieved from http://www.medicalnewstoday.com/articles/

INFORMATIVE SPEECH | PLANNING FORM

Name: _____ Topic: _____

1 | Write a specific purpose statement for your proposed topic.

2 | Write a thesis statement for your proposed topic. Remember, this should be one complete and declarative sentence.

3 | Clearly state how your topic is relevant to your audience (e.g., What might they gain from listening to it? Why should they care?).

4 | What makes YOU credible to speak on this topic? (e.g., How much time have you researched? What is your background on the topic? Where did you gain your information?)

5 | Which organizational pattern do you think you will use for this speech? (Time-Sequence, Spatial, Topical, or Cause-Effect)

6 | With this organizational pattern in mind list three main points you could cover for this speech.

   A |

   B |

   C |

7 | Now choose a different organizational pattern. With this organizational pattern in mind list three main points you could cover for this speech.

   A |

   B |

   C |

8 | Which organizational pattern and main points do you believe will best reach your audience?

Now that your organizational pattern and main points have been chosen:

9 | What are three goals for the research process? (Consider how you hope to conduct research or learn more about your topic, what sources you may need to find, etc.)

   A |

   B |

   C |

10 | List three different sources that you plan to include in the speech. Your sources should include at least three of the following: books; newspaper, magazine, Internet or research articles and; interviews or television news stories. You may NOT use Wikipedia.

   A |

   B |

   C |

PEER EVALUATION OF INFORMATIVE SPEECH ASSIGNMENT

Your Name: _____

Speaker's Name: _____ Topic: _____

Use this legend to understand the quality of your classmate's performance in each category.

"+" Well Done   "o" Okay/Average   " – " Needs Improvement   "×" Not Included

_____ **Introduction**

_____ Attention getter
_____ Established relevance
_____ Established credibility
_____ Clear thesis statement
_____ Included preview

_____ **Body**

_____ Effective organization
_____ Support/evidence
_____ Clear transitions

_____ **Conclusion**

_____ Reviewed main points
_____ Restated thesis statement
_____ Ended speech strongly

_____ **Delivery**

_____ Effective vocal delivery
_____ Used hand gestures well
_____ Maintained eye contact
_____ Used extemporaneous style
_____ Used notecards effectively

Written Comments

Three Things the Speaker did Well:

Three Things to Improve:

CRITERIA FOR EVALUATING INFORMATIVE SPEECHES

Introduction *15 Points Possible*

Gained Attention	**(C)** = Prepared audience to listen **(B)** = and creates a need to listen **(A)** = and is original & creative.
Made Topic Relevant	**(C)** = Established importance of topic **(B)** = and relates the topic to audience **(A)** = and is significant to the audience.
Established Credibility	**(C)** = Student states why she/he is credible to speak on the topic **(B)** = and is a logical argument for the speaker **(A)** = and is unique & creative.
Stated Thesis Clearly	**(C)** = Statement is clear & direct **(B)** = and it flows logically to the preview **(A)** = and it reflects a unique & creative approach to the topic.
Stated Preview Clearly	**(C)** = Statement outlines main points **(B)** = and flows from the thesis **(A)** = and uses original and creative language.

Body *30 Points Possible*

Main Points Clear	**(C)** = Main points are easily identifiable **(B)** = and each main point is an independent idea **(A)** = and main points are set-up previews and signposts.
Strong Evidence & Support	**(C)** = Minimum of 5 sources are orally cited **(B)** = and links between sources and main points are clear **(A)** = and there is evidence of analysis and understanding.
Organization Effective	**(C)** = Arrangement of main points is appropriate **(B)** = and meets the purpose of the speech **(A)** = and is clearly constructed with creative language.
Used Precise, Clear, & Descriptive Language	**(C)** = Language is appropriate **(B)** = and language is predominantly concrete **(A)** = and language is vivid, creative, and utilizes imagery or metaphors.

Conclusion *10 Points Possible*

Restated Thesis	**(C)** = Thesis is clearly stated **(B)** = and flows with a transition from the body of the speech **(A)** = and flows with a transition to the review of main points.
Reviewed Main Points	**(C)** = Briefly reviewed all main points **(B)** = and transitions are used **(A)** = and it is different from the preview statement in the introduction.
Made Presentation Memorable	**(C)** = Topic was adapted to audience **(B)** = and the speech made references to the audience **(A)** = and the speech considered the audience's thinking about the topic.

Delivery *20 Points Possible*

Used Vocal Variety	**(C)** = Some vocal variety used during parts of the speech **(B)** = and vocal variety is used to highlight ideas **(A)** = and the speaker uses voice, rate, and diction to demonstrate interest in the speech.
Used Appropriate Articulation/ Pronunciation	**(C)** = There are 3 or more mis-articulated or mispronounced words **(B)** = There are 3 or fewer mis-articulated or mispronounced correctly **(A)** = All words are articulated and pronounced correctly.
Established Eye Contact With the Audience	**(C)** = Maintained eye contact with the audience **(B)** = and the student is able to move between looking at the audience and the notecard **(A)** = and gages feedback from the audience for a majority of the time.
Used Appropriate Gestures, Body Movement, & Facial Expressions	**(C)** = Some distracting gestures, body movement or facial expressions. **(B)** = Gestures, body movement, and facial expressions add emphasis. **(A)** = Gestures, body movement, and facial expressions are used to demonstrate enthusiasm for the speech.

Use the following notations to evaluate your classmate's speech:
"+" Well Done   "o" Okay/Average   "–" Needs Improvement   "×" Not Included

INSTRUCTOR EVALUATION OF INFORMATIVE SPEECH ASSIGNMENT

Speaker's Name: _____ Total Points: _____ /100

Time Infraction: _____ Time: _____

Use this legend to understand the quality of your performance in each category.

"+" Well Done   "o" Okay/Average   " – " Needs Improvement   "×" Not Included

_____ **Introduction   (15 points)**
_____ Gained attention
_____ Made topic relevant
_____ Established credibility
_____ Stated thesis clearly
_____ Stated preview clearly

_____ **Body   (30 points)**
_____ Main points clear
_____ Strong evidence/support
_____ Organization effective
_____ Used precise, clear, and descriptive language

_____ **Conclusion   (10 points)**
_____ Restated thesis
_____ Reviewed main points
_____ Made presentation memorable

_____ **Organization   (5 points)**
_____ Main points organized in proper sequence building to action
_____ Main points broken down into sub-pts
_____ Organized well (transitions, internal summaries, flows well)
_____ Main points were developed evenly

_____ **Supporting Material   (10 points)**
_____ Quality of supporting material (examples, statistics, quotations)
_____ Appropriate sources
_____ Cited at least five appropriate sources

_____ **Delivery   (20 points)**
_____ Used vocal variety (pitch, rate, volume)
_____ Used appropriate articulation/pronunciation
_____ Used minimal vocal disfluencies
_____ Established eye contact with audience
_____ Used appropriate gestures and body movement, facial expressions

Speeches have a 15 second grace period over/under time limit without penalty. Speeches that go 16–29 seconds over/under the time limit will be reduced by 3 points. Speeches that go 30 seconds over/under the time limit will be reduced by 5 points. Excessive time infraction can result in larger penalty per discretion of Instructor.

Outline and References   (10 points)

_____ Narrowed and focused
_____ Reflected presentation
_____ Used proper outline format (including transitions, full sentence structure, and correct grammar and spelling)
_____ Credibility of sources
_____ At least five sources included in bibliography
_____ Sources cited throughout the outline in APA Format
_____ References in APA format
_____ Submitted to safe-assign

Presentation Strengths:

Areas for Improvement:

Chapter 12 FINDING AND EVALUATING SOURCES

BY JEFF KUZNEKOFF*

*We would like to thank Jessica Hagman, OU Reference Librarian, for her helpful
feedback on this chapter. Michelle Calka, Valerie Lynn Schrader, Heather M. Stassen,
and Abbey Wojno also contributed to earlier versions of this chapter.

FINDING AND EVALUATING SOURCES

In this chapter, you will learn how to use library research to find good sources for your speech. You will also learn how to evaluate the quality of those sources. This will be beneficial as you will learn how to properly cite sources in APA format in-text and for your Reference page in subsequent chapters. Both the informative and persuasive speeches require you to do research and this entails finding and integrating credible outside sources into your speech. If you are panicking about the research process, don't! It does take time, but many resources are available to help you. As your textbook outlines, students typically use four primary types of sources in their speeches: personal experience, interviews, library resources, and web sources. This section will focus on Alden Library's academic and popular press library resources as well as web sources that are appropriate for this course.

RESOURCES FOR COMS 1030

We are lucky to have a website specifically designed to help COMS 1030 students with research for speeches (*http://libguides.library.ohiou.edu/coms1030*). OU Reference Librarian Jessica Hagman created this library guide specifically for our course, and it is an excellent place to start your research for your speech. The COMS 1030 library guide contains examples for possible speech topics, links to suggested research sources for your speech, video tips on using library resources, and contact information for Alden Library staff in case you have questions.

LIBRARY RESOURCES

Ohio University's Alden Library has an amazing amount of journals, news media, and books available both on and off-campus. On the Alden Library home page (*http://www. library.ohiou.edu/*) you will find a variety of resources to help you conduct your research. The best starting place is the search box for the ArticlesPlus database. This search box is displayed on the main page of the library website. The ArticlesPlus database searches for books, news sources, and academic journals using the search terms you entered. After you perform a search, using your own keywords or terms, you can limit the results of your search to specific types of sources and by publication date. For example, if you enter the term "Global Warming" and perform a search, you can then limit the results by selecting academic journals, periodicals, news, books, or ebooks. In addition, you could also limit your search to results that have been published between 2005 and 2015. By limiting the results of your search to specific types, and even publication dates, you can more easily refine your search parameters and find credible sources for your speech.

Types of Sources

1 | Books and Ebooks

Books are some of the most useful sources of information for helping you build your speech. Using the ArticlesPlus search (explained above), you can narrow your search results to look for books and ebooks. The ArticlesPlus database contains information on both paper and electronic books available through the library. After you have done a search for a topic in ArticlesPlus, check the box for Books and/or eBooks in the Source Types limiter on the left side of the page and then click update. Once you find a book that looks useful, click on the title to find out more about that book and whether a copy is available in the library. Ebooks should be accessible directly through the ArticlesPlus database.

Often students will use Google or another search engine to quickly find information online. Although search engines are very good at finding information quickly, they are also bad at helping you evaluate those sources. The best option for COMS 1030 is to avoid search engines, for the time being, and focus your search using ArticlesPlus.

CAUTION

2 | News Sources

Many public speaking students find newspaper and magazine articles to be the most accessible type of research for their topic. The ArticlesPlus database includes news sources from national and local newspapers, and after you have done a search in ArticlesPlus, you can limit your results to these types of articles by checking the box for News under the Source Types limiter and then clicking update.

For example, if you are researching the topic of tuition increases across the state of Ohio, one of the best sources of information will be news sources. Using ArticlesPlus, you can use search terms that you think relate to this topic and limit your results to only news sources. In addition, you can use the slider on the left to select news sources from 2008–2012, so that you are focusing your search on more recent articles.

3 | Academic Journal Articles

Perhaps one of the most credible sources is an academic journal article. Academic journal articles are scholarly sources that are based on systematic research. Most of the academic journal articles that will be useful for you are research studies, which use rigorous methods like experiments, extended case studies, large surveys, or other established ways to answer specific research questions. They are different from news sources because academic journal articles are based on a long and systematic research process. Because research takes a long time to do, academic journal articles may not be as timely as news sources. But they can offer strong evidence to support the claims in your speech.

Another reason academic journal articles are considered to be highly credible is that journal articles typically undergo a rigorous review prior to publication. During this review process, an author submits an anonymous manuscript to a journal editor. The editor then sends out this anonymous manuscript to several reviewers. These reviewers are experts in the field of study and/or the specific content area covered in that manuscript. The expert reviewers, who are also anonymous, read through the manuscript and submit their feedback to the editor, who then decides if the manuscript needs a little more work, is ready for publication, or should be rejected. This process is known as *peer review* and allows academic journals to thoroughly vet academic work to maintain high scholarly standards.

To find academic journal articles in ArticlesPlus, use the Source Types limit on the left side of the search results page. Check the box for Academic Journals (or scholarly peer reviewed) and click update. In addition, you can also select a range for the year of publication in case you want to limit your results to specific years. For example, let's say that you are researching how the use of Facebook impacts student's impressions of teachers. Doing a simple news search provides a few news articles; however, you want to find more credible sources. Using ArticlesPlus, you can use the same search terms but limit the results to scholarly, peer reviewed articles. In the case of this topic, you will be able to find several journal articles that discuss scholarly research that has examined this topic in detail.

4 | World Wide Web

The last major type of source regularly used in public speeches are World Wide Web or simply web sources. To put it simply, web sources are those sources that only exist online and do not have print counterparts. For example, a company website is a web source, since it does not have a print version of the website, but the electronic copy of a print document (like a newspaper article) is not considered a web source, since it was printed first but also available online. In general, the following are the most common types of web sources used in most public speeches:

- Company/commercial websites (often ending in .com)
- Special interest/nonprofit websites (often ending in .org)
- Professional websites
- Government websites (ending in .gov)
- University websites (ending in .edu)

Using the right type of web source is an important step in evaluating your sources. For example, if you are writing a speech about the rising cost of a college education, you might cite information from Ohio University's financial aid page about tuition increases over the last decade. However, you might want to avoid using someone's personal blog posting, especially if they do not cite their sources or use questionable information. In addition, some websites are not frequently updated and thus can display inaccurate or outdated information. One way of avoiding this pitfall is by using information from those web sources that have an established history of being a credible source.

EVALUATING SOURCES

After you have found potential sources for your speech, you will need to evaluate the quality of your sources and how credible the information contained in that source is. Below are criteria that can be applied to judge the quality of a source. The criteria listed are general considerations, but keep in mind that you may need to adjust the criteria depending on your chosen speech topic.

1 | Clarity

Is the information provided clear and easy to understand? Does the source provide information at a level your audience will be able to understand? Keep in mind that you should have selected a topic that you already know something about, but you should be aware that your audience may not have the same level of knowledge about the topic. Select sources that your audience will be able to understand. For example, if you are writing a speech on the White House, you should avoid complex sources that discuss the architectural complexities of the White House. Rather, you should select sources that discuss the history and general layout of the White House.

2 | Reliability

Has this source been correct in the past? Based on past experiences, can you depend on this source to provide you with accurate information? If you answered yes to both of the above questions, there is a good chance that the source is reliable. Using reputable newspapers such as *The Wall Street Journal* or *The New York Times* is a good option for your speech because these sources engage in fact-checking. For example, when gathering sources for a speech on U.S. foreign policy with North Korea, you should refer to a nationally recognized newspaper, like the *International Herald Tribune,* or wire service as opposed to an article from a regional newspaper, like the *Columbus Dispatch.*

3 | Credibility

What formal education or experience does the source have regarding this subject (expertise)? Do you believe this person or source is apt to tell you the truth (trustworthiness)? Does this source have the audience's best interests in mind (goodwill)? Do you feel that the source believes in his or her own information (dynamism)? While lay (non-expert) or celebrity testimony is useful as a method of support, you should also include information from sources that have significant experience with your topic. Peer reviewed academic journal articles are written by experts in the field and will provide you with credible information on your topic. For example, testimony from Britney Spears on a speech about animal rights would not be a good source. A better source would be an article that discusses the current treatment of farm animals.

4 | Objectivity

Is the source biased in some way? Does the bias complicate or call into question the accuracy or reliability of the information provided? If you answered yes to both questions, you should reconsider your source. If you feel that your source is biased, you should try to find a more objective source that confirms the information. For instance, statistics about the harmful effects of smoking from a study that was funded by a tobacco company should be confirmed elsewhere. When using websites or a research study, you should take into consideration who paid for the study and what their interests are in the topic. For example if you were to give a speech on GARDASIL, a vaccination for the HPV Virus, the GARDASIL website would not be the best source to use because the website is promoting the product. A better source to use would be the Federal Drug Administration's report on GARDASIL.

5 | Applicability/Relevancy

Is this source directly related to your topic? While it is important to find sources that directly relate to your topic, you should also be careful not to limit your search too narrowly. You should not feel as though you are "stretching" your information to make it fit within your speech. When preparing for a speech that discusses melanoma, an article that directly discusses skin cancer would be a better source than an article that discusses cancer in general.

6 | Timeliness

Does the source contain the most current information? If the source is not from within the past five years, why do you feel that the source is still relevant to your topic? In a constantly changing world, it is important that you have located the most current information. Having up-to-date sources will increase the audience's perception of your own credibility. For a speech on the 2012 Olympics in London, a recent article that reflects on the event would be better than an older article that announces that London was selected to be the host city.

FINDING SOURCES | EXERCISE

Name: _____

What is your speech topic? _____

Now that you have your topic, it is time to use what we learned to find sources from Alden Library. For this speech you will need at least three sources, which you should locate using Alden Library's ArticlesPlus or the COMS 1030 library guide. You will need a World Wide Web source, a news source, and a source of your Instructor's choosing. Do the following:

1 | First, find a World Wide Web source that speaks to your topic. Write down the URL and the name of the organization and/or person responsible for the source.

How will you use the information from the World Wide Web source in your speech? Bring to class a copy of the information that you will be using from the World Wide Web source.

2 | Second, find a news source that speaks to your topic. Below write down the title of the article, author name, date and year of publication, and title of the publication.

How will you use the information from the news source in your speech? Bring to class a copy of the article.

3 | Finally, find a third source (of your Instructor's choosing) that provides information that you can use in your speech. Below write down any information (title, author, etc.) that would enable someone to easily locate your source.

How will you use the information from the source in your speech? Bring to class a copy of the information that you will be using from this source.

SOURCE EVALUATION EXERCISE

Now that you have completed the Finding Sources Exercise and located a World Wide Web source, a news source, and a third source of your Instructor's choosing, it is time to evaluate each of your three sources. Please type your evaluation and turn in a copy of your answers to your Instructor on the assigned due date.

WORLD WIDE WEB SOURCE

1 | Using APA style, provide the citation for the World Wide Web source.

2 | In a paragraph, explain why you feel that this is a good source for your speech. In evaluating your source, consider the criteria for source evaluation in this chapter. Some questions might include:

A | In what ways are the information appropriate for a classroom audience?

B | Why do you feel that the source is reliable?

C | In what ways are the source credible? How, if at all, is the source biased? If there is a bias, how will this bias be tempered in your speech?

D | Was the World Wide Web source updated recently? If no, please explain why you feel this source is still timely.

POPULAR PRESS SOURCE

1 | Using APA style, provide the citation for the news article.

2 | In a paragraph, explain why you feel that this is a good source for your speech. In evaluating your source, consider the criteria for source evaluation in this chapter. Some questions might include:

A | In what ways are the information appropriate for a classroom audience?

B | Why do you feel that the popular press article is reliable?

C | In what ways are the article credible? How, if at all, is the article biased? If there is a bias, how will this bias be tempered in your speech?

D | Why do you feel that this article is timely?

THIRD SOURCE

1 | Using APA style, provide the citation for the "Instructor's choice" source.

2 | In a paragraph, explain why you feel that this is a good source for your speech. In evaluating your source, consider the criteria for source evaluation in this chapter. Some questions might include:

A | In what ways are the information appropriate for a classroom audience?

B | Why do you feel that this source is reliable?

C | In what ways are the source credible?

D | How, if at all, is the source biased?

E | If there is a bias, how will this bias be tempered in your speech?

F | Why do you feel that this source is timely?

Chapter 13 APA GUIDELINES

BY ZAMZAM JAMA AND KATY A. ROSS*

APA GUIDELINES

As a student in COMS 1030 you are required to cite each source you use in your presentations. Now that you found and evaluated your sources, the next step is to integrate the information form the sources into your speech outline and attribute those sources during your actual speech. One critical step in this process is telling your audience or reader where the information originally came from. This is called citing your sources.

This chapter presents the importance of properly citing your sources in APA format. For COMS 1030, each student will cite sources in three different ways: **oral citations, in-text citations, and reference list citations.** In this chapter we will look at guidelines and samples to help you do all three approaches. The examples can be used to help you create your own citations. Finally, we encourage you to use the interactive checklist to ensure you have completed all of the necessary steps to using proper APA formatting for your reference page.

CAUTIONARY MESSAGE

The COMS 1030 course policy requires proper written citations to be used when referencing work that is not your own original work in your presentation outlines and other written work. If not followed, this policy can deem your work plagiarism, which could result in a zero and/or a report to the Dean of Students.

In addition, you must orally (i.e., verbally) cite sources during the actual delivery of your speech. At minimum state the author, date of publication, publication information when using the sources in your outline during the delivery of your presentations.

BENEFICIARY MESSAGE

Three benefits from properly citing your sources:

1 | You allow the person who put in the hard work to receive proper credit.

2 | You are more credible because you show you have done your research on the topic.

3 | You have a better understanding of how the research process works.

ORAL CITATION

As your textbook explains, oral citations tell the listener who the source is, how recent the information is, and the source's qualifications. Your textbook provides some examples of oral citations. Let's take a closer look to see how these examples reference the source of the information, the date the information was made public, and the qualifications of the source.

"According to a 2008 interview with clinical psychologist Dina Zeckhausen, founder of the Eating Disorders Information Network, mothers are influential in their daughters' understanding of healthy body images."

"Dr. Elizabeth Graham, a family communication researcher at Ohio University, found in a 2003 study that relationships go through several contradictory trends after a divorce."

Who is the source?	How recent is the information?	What are the source's qualifications
Dina Zeckhausen in the interview	2008	A clinical psychologist and founder of the Eating Disorders Information Network
Dr. Elizabeth Graham in the study	2003	A family communication researcher at Ohio University

When orally citing web pages, there is no need to indicate the URL web address. Spelling out "www.orphanage-outreach.org" will distract from your presentation. In order to keep the focus on your message, simply share with your audience the title of the web page or the name of the organization that supports the website.

You must also indicate the date that the information on the web page was posted. Here's an example:

"The Orphanage Outreach website, updated in May of 2008, states that over 5,000 individuals have volunteered with Orphanage Outreach in Dominican Republic since 1994."

No matter the source, it is important to orally cite all information that is not general knowledge or your own unique thought. Please make sure to give credit where credit is due. Failing to orally cite information or claiming information as your own constitutes academic dishonesty. If you have any questions or concerns about properly citing information please feel free to ask your Instructor for assistance.

1 | Books

The correct APA format for references to books is:

Author. (Date). *Name of book.* Place book was published: Publishing company.

Here are some examples:

One Author

Black, T. R. (1999). *Doing quantitative research in the social sciences.* Thousand Oaks, CA: Sage.

Several Authors

Hammerback, J. C., & Jensen, R. J. (1998). *The rhetorical career of Cesar Chavez.* College Station, TX: Texas A&M University Press.

Chapter in an Edited Book

If you are using a chapter from an edited book, you will need to cite a little more information. Often the person who wrote the chapter you are citing is different from the person who edited the whole book. So, instead of just citing the book, you will need to list the authors of the chapter, the title of the chapter, the editors of the book, the title of the book, the pages the chapter appears on, and the publisher information. Be sure to italicize the title of the book, not the title of the specific chapter. For example,

Welser, H. T., Smith, M., Fisher, D., & Gleave, E. (2008). Distilling digital traces: Computational social science approaches to studying the Internet. In N. Fielding, R. M. Lee and G. Blank (Eds.), *Handbook of online research methods* (pp. 116–140). London: Sage.

2 | Academic Journal Article

The correct APA format for academic journal article references is:

Author. (Date). Title of article. *Name of journal, Volume number,* Page numbers.

Here are some examples:

One Author

Benoit, W. L. (2003). Topic of presidential campaign discourse and election outcome. *Western Journal of Communication, 67,* 97–112.

Multiple Authors

Mazer, J. P., Murphy, R. E., & Simonds, C. J. (2007). I'll see you on "Facebook": The effects of computer-mediated teacher self-disclosure on student motivation, affective learning, and classroom climate. *Communication Education, 56,* 1–17.

3 | News Source

The correct APA format for news source references is:

Author. (Date). Name of article. *Name of periodical, Volume number,* Page numbers.

There is some variation depending on where you got the news source (print or online) and whether the article's author is listed. Here are some examples:

Basic format for News Source

Szczesny, J. R. (2005, August 8). 10 questions for Andrew Stern. *Time, 16, 6.*

News Source Accessed Online

If you retrieve the news article from a newspaper's website, then you need to include the URL instead of page numbers. Do not include the link for the search engine or database (i.e., ArticlesPlus), that just describes how you found the source. Instead, include the direct URL to the article on the newspaper's webpage.

Dewitt, D. (2012, June 13). City may act to reign in student street fests. *The Athens News.* Retrieved from http://www.athensnews.com/ohio.

News Source with No Author Listed

In the event that your article has no author, put the title of the article where the author's name would typically be.

Labor Splits. (2005, August 15). *Nation, 281,* 4.

4 | World Wide Web Source

The correct APA format for a web source references is:

Author or Organization. (Posted or Updated Date). *Title of website.* Retrieved from followed by the URL

For example:

Centers for Disease Control and Prevention. (2010). *2009 H1N1 flu.* Retrieved from http://www.cdc.gov

5 | Interviews , Email, and Other Personal Communication

(E. Chimes, personal communication, January 7, 2015).

IN-TEXT CITATIONS IN WRITING

Why Do We Use In-Text Citations?

In COMS 1030, we want you to develop your arguments by finding and using credible sources to support your ideas. In-text citations allow a reader to know where you found your sources and how you used them. For example, if you found a source you want to use for your first body point, you must find a way to signal to the reader that there is a credible source who agrees with your perspective. The way to do this is to use APA format for in-text citations. By placing an APA citation at the end of your direct quote or paraphrase, in your outline or papers, the reader will be able to discern the evidence used to support your claim.

In-text citations are used any time an idea or words from a source are used. Keep in mind: If you read the information somewhere, you have to cite that information. It is important to give credit to the original authors. Otherwise, you're stealing their idea that they worked hard to get published.

Direct Quote versus Paraphrase

A *direct quotation* is used when citing a source word for word or using seven or more consecutive words at a time from the source. This usually shows that you are using the direct words of the author to portray an argument or to make a claim. Direct quotations are accompanied with quotation marks around the information and page numbers in the citation in your outline or paper.

A *paraphrased statement* is used to summarize the words of an author or work. It should be framed in the words of the writer; this means you! Paraphrasing is when you put the source's ideas into your own words, and it does not require quotation marks in your outline or paper. However, since the idea was not yours originally, credit must be given to the original author using in-text citations at the end of the sentence in your outline or paper.

EXAMPLES

Works by a Single Author

Direct Quotation

According to Petronio (2002), "Role risks are those that have the potential to jeopardize our standing if we disclose private information" (p. 71).

> Or it could be written like this:

"Role risks are those that have the potential to jeopardize our standing in if we disclose private information" (Petronio, 2002, p. 71).

Paraphrase Statement

Individuals assess the potential risks and benefits before they decide to self disclose information (Petronio, 2002).

> Or it could be written like this:

According to Petronio (2002), individuals assess the potential risks and benefits before they decide to self disclose information.

Note: There are no page numbers needed for paraphrase quotes because you are paraphrasing from the author.

Works by Multiple Authors

Direct Quotation

"In terms of student-Instructor relationships, students viewed their instructors as more immediate when they used Twitter" (DiVerniero & Hosek, 2013, p. 69).

Paraphrase Statement

Students feel closer to teachers that use twitter (DiVerniero & Hosek, 2013).

Note: You must use an ampersand (&) between authors. When you have six or more authors your in-text format should include "et al." after the first author.

Works by Associations, Corporations, or Government Agencies

Direct Quotation

"The federal Workforce Investment Act (WIA) provides federal funds to states for job training and employment services" (Department of Job and Family Services [DJFS], 2008, p. 7).

Paraphrase Statement

In the United States, federal funding provides career assistance for individuals seeking employment (Department of Job and Family Services [DJFS], 2008).

Works with No Author

Direct Quotation

"Step Up To Quality was created by the Ohio Department of Job & Family Services—Bureau of Child Care and Development to improve the quality of child care in Ohio" ("Athens County Child," 2009, p. 9).

Paraphrase Statement

In Ohio there are government services that help families and children ("Athens County Child," 2009).

Works with No Date

Direct Quotation

"Ohio University is committed to maintaining a safe environment in which students can pursue their academic and personal goals" ("Ohio University Guide," n.d.).

Paraphrase Statement

Ohio University upholds standards of civility ("Ohio University Guide," n.d.).

REFERENCE LIST

Tip: Why Do We Use a Reference List?

A reference list is used to allow readers to locate a resource for more information. The reference list is a page(s) and includes a list of all of the sources you have used to create your speech outline. Ideally, your readers will be interested in what you choose to present and will want to read more about your topic (i.e., *information hunger*). By providing a reference list, your readers are able to find more information about your topic via the specific sources you used.

Proper in-text citations are meant to be a shorthand version of the full citation, which belongs in your reference list. The reader knows to look in the reference list to find the full citation when they see the in-text citation in your outline.

Tip: Where Does the Reference List Go?

Your reference list should appear at the end of your outline/paper (unless otherwise indicated in the assignment's guidelines or by your Instructor). It provides the information necessary for a reader to locate and retrieve any source you cite in the body of the outline/paper. **Each source you cite orally or in-text must appear in your reference list; likewise, each entry in the reference list must be cited in your outline/orally.**

Your references should begin on a new page separate from the text of the essay; label this page "References" centered at the top of the page in **Bold** (do NOT underline, or use quotation marks for the title).

Tip: How Do You Create a Hanging Indent?

All lines after the first line of each entry in your reference list should be indented one-half inch from the left margin. This is called **hanging indentation.**

A hanging indent helps your reference list look visually appealing and creates more organization overall. There are two options to include hanging indents for each reference and both are PC and Mac friendly.

Option One
1 | Make sure your cursor is on the first line.
2 | Go to the "Format" tab and click on "Paragraph."
3 | In the "Indents and Spacing" tab on this box you will see the section labeled "Indentations."
4 | Within this section there is a dropdown box for "Special."
5 | Click on this dropdown box and choose "Hanging."
6 | All of the lines in your citation, except for the first one, should indent together.
7 | Repeat for each citation.

Option Two
1 | Make sure your cursor is on the line you want to indent.
2 | Hold down the "Control" button and press the "Tab" button.
3 | You will need to repeat this for each individual line of each citation.

Tip: What Rules Govern How Authors Are Listed?

- Reference list entries should be alphabetized by the last name of the first author of each work.

- Authors' names are inverted (last name first); write out the last name and initials for all authors of a particular work for up to and including seven authors. If the work has more than seven authors, list the first six authors and then use ellipses after the sixth author's name. After the ellipses, list the last author's name of the work.

- If you have more than one article by the same author, single-author references or multiple-author references with the exact same authors in the exact same order are listed in order by the year of publication, starting with the earliest.

Tip: What Gets Capitalized and Italicized in Journal Articles and in Books?

- Capitalize all major words in journal titles and italicize the journal title. For example: *The Journal of Family Communication*.

- When referring to books, chapters, article titles, or Web pages, capitalize only the first letter of the first word of a title and subtitle, the first word after a colon or a dash in the title, and proper nouns.

- Italicize titles of books but remember the tip above when doing so.

REFERENCE LIST REQUIRED FORMATTING CHECKLIST

- ☐ Are your references in alphabetical order?
- ☐ Do you have a hanging indent for each citation?
- ☐ Are your references double-spaced?
- ☐ Do you have the title "References" centered and bolded?
- ☐ Have you removed the color and underline of the hyperlink for websites?
- ☐ Is your reference list on a separate page (unless being used for your speech outline)?
- ☐ Did you put (n.d.) for the sources that have no publication date?

EXTRA RESOURCES

It is certainly possible you will still have questions after following the format laid out in this chapter. For specific questions, you can ask your Instructor for help. Before you go to your Instructor though, try doing some searching on your own for the answers to your questions.

There are many good online references for helping you appropriately format your references, such as the Citations Section of our COMS 1030 library guide. Another excellent source on the APA style is *www.owl.english.purdue.edu*. This site provides you with the guidelines for both in-text citations and reference lists and it also provides examples of papers with correct APA format.

Chapter 14 ARGUMENT DEVELOPMENT: FRAMING YOUR IDEAS

BY KEITH C. BISTODEAU

ARGUMENT DEVELOPMENT FRAMING YOUR IDEAS

INTRODUCTION

For most students in college, public speaking is one of their biggest fears, if not their biggest fear (Walton, 2005). In part, one reason for this is because students struggle with forming and clearly expressing their ideas in a public speaking situation. The difficult task of forming ideas in a clear and supported manner is the aim of this chapter. And so, this chapter will draw upon Stephen Toulmin's (1958) model of argument as a means of providing you the tools to not only research your topics better, but to provide you a means of better structuring and expressing your ideas. To do this, we will review the elements of Toulmin's model, describe ways you can use the model in COMS 1030, clarify how the model will increase your confidence while speaking, and illustrate how the model can be used in other contexts outside of COMS 1030.

ELEMENTS OF TOULMIN'S MODEL

Toulmin created his model to help people better create and understand arguments. The model contains four elements: data, claim, warrant, and backing. There are two additional elements *qualifiers and rebuttals* that are beyond the scope of COMS 1030, but you can take additional courses in argumentation to learn more about those elements. Many individuals who speak professionally (or competitively like our own OU Speaking Bobcats) have training in using this model. The reason for this is simple, it works! For COMS 1030 you will need to know four parts of the model: claim, data, warrant, and backing.

Claim

A claim can be thought of as your thesis. This is the **guiding idea** that you are attempting to convey to your audience during your speech. For example, if you felt that college students need to get a certain amount of sleep per night and you found data to back up that idea, you could form the following claim: Ohio University should not have classes before 9:00 a.m. because college students need at least eight hours of sleep to be successful in the classroom.

Data

Data is the information that you find during your research process that will help you support your claims during your speech. Although claims come first in the model, **this is actually where you should start in the model because the data (i.e., research) will help to guide how you structure your claims.** Without strong data the rest of your argument may not be complete, compelling, or credible. If you were creating a speech to remove classes before 9:00 a.m., you could find source that shows how the human brain needs a certain amount of sleep, or how the brain works at different times of the day, or how the class schedules and demands of the college lifestyle make it difficult to do well in early morning classes.

Warrant

Warrant can be thought of as the social support for your claim. If there are socially held views and beliefs that are similar to your claims, they can be used to help support your data and your claim. If we think about the example above you can probably think of conversations and social stances that support individuals needing a certain amount of sleep each night. Warrants also help you to explain your data and why it is important because warrants help to justify your information and claims.

If you use conversations and social stance, make sure to have sources you can reference to back up your statements. Yes, public opinions and beliefs matter, but you need to have research to support your ideas and add to your credibility as a speaker. A good rule of thumb to follow is that if you use a social claim you should pair it with a cited source.

Backing

Backing is the support and justification that helps to back up your warrant. You could use interviews or articles found during your data collection to help set up the backing for your claim(s) and warrant for your speech. You can think of backing as the glue that holds your claim(s) together. Backing is interdependent with data, meaning that the two elements work together in speeches and during the speech writing process. A good way to understand the difference between data and backing is that data is your primary information but the backing is the link to your claim. If you cannot justify the data you are using or the claim you are making, your argument may not be compelling, informative, or persuasive.

USING TOULMIN'S MODEL IN COMS 1030

While the focus of COMS 1030 is on giving presentations, effective research is required in order for your speeches to perceived as credible, ethical, and successful in the class. In part, Toulmin's (1958) model can assist you in achieving those goals. More specifically, Toulmin's model can help you in three ways: (a) when you are conducting research for your speeches, (b) when you are crafting/creating the content your speeches, and (c) when you are preparing for/delivering your speeches in class.

Conducting Research for Your Speeches

When conducting research on a topic for a speech it is sometimes difficult to figure out where you want to start. Toulmin's (1958) model provides a template for you to use when finding and evaluating sources. When looking for data for your speech you can check to see if the data supports the general ideas you have for your claim(s). If it does not, you probably should not use that source. This will not only help to speed up the research process, but will also help you craft stronger claim(s).

Crafting Content for Your Speeches

Once you have finished researching your topic you need to start writing your speech outline. For COMS 1030 you are required to craft a formal full-sentence outline of your speech and submit the outline before you deliver your speech in class. Toulmin's (1958) model functions as a checklist for you during this process. As you are writing out your formal sentence outline you can refer to the model to verify that your ideas follow the model and that all of your ideas are supported and clear. This will help you write the outline and should help limit the number of edits you have to make during the writing process.

Speech Delivery

The last part of the speech process in COMS 1030 is delivering your speech in class. When you follow the Toulmin (1958) model with your research and while writing your speech, the delivery component is much easier. Because the Toulmin model trains you to structure your ideas in a logical manner it is easier for you to communicate your speech and for your audience to follow your speech. When the elements of Toulmin's Model can be identified in your speech this improves the overall organization of your speech and increases the fluidity of your delivery.

HOW TOULMIN'S MODEL INCREASES SPEAKING CONFIDENCE

Increasing your confidence as a speaker is one of the primary goals of COMS 1030. The course is structured in a way that allows you to have ample practice with giving presentations in front of an audience. In all, understanding and using Toulmin's (1958) model builds confidence, over time, both during and after your complete COMS 1030.

For the sake of COMS 1030, the model will help to improve your confidence as a speaker in three ways: (a) the model will help to make you a better researcher when you are preparing your speeches, (b) the model will help you construct better arguments when preparing your speeches, and (c) the model will help you have better delivery when you are presenting your speeches in class.

Better Research

When conducting research for a speech it is important to make sure that your data clearly supports your claims. Toulmin's (1958) model helps to ensure that this occurs. Since the model asks you to consider all four elements of the model throughout the entire speech development process, your ability to find good information increases with an understanding of the model. As stated above, the model functions almost like a checklist for you during this part of the process. Here's a simple phrase to remember: **Better research leads to better arguments, and better arguments lead to better delivery.**

Better Arguments

The arguments (claims) you make in your speech are the key points of the speaking process. These are the components of your speech that you want to clearly convey to your audience. If you do not have arguments that are strong and clear it will be difficult for your audience to follow your train of thought and to understand and agree with what you are saying. The Toulmin (1958) model helps you craft better arguments because the model makes you consider multiple perspectives of an issue when you are crafting your speech. The more that you know about a subject, the better arguments you can make.

Better Delivery

The last area that the Toulmin (1958) model helps you with in COMS 1030 is with the delivery of your speech. If you used the model to help with your research and argument construction, it will carry over to helping with your delivery during your speech. The model helps you to frame your ideas in a manner that is easy to explain and say out loud. This is one of the key parts about this model. It not only helps you during the construction of the speech, but also when you are delivering the speech in class.

While Toulmin's model helps with construction and delivery of speeches, it also helps you to identify different types of speeches. Not every speech is constructed the same way, nor do they sound the same. The next section helps to further illustrate how the Toulmin model can be used for different types of speeches.

SPEECHES OF FACT, VALUE, AND POLICY

Every speaking situation calls for different research and methods of connecting to an audience. This is something that every speaker, regardless of level of experience, struggles with. The three main claims you can use to frame your speeches are: arguments based on facts, values, and on policy.

Argument of Fact

The first way you can approach a speaking situation is to focus on making claims to/from facts. This means that your speech would focus on the existence of or definition of a situation, individual, or event. By using facts you are referencing ideas or concepts that support your claims. An example of this could be a speech on recycling that uses recycling and waste statistics for the Athens area.

Argument of Value

The second type of argument you can use is a value-based argument. This means that you are making your claim based upon tastes or morals, or if something is good or bad. Think of this as a speech from social beliefs or ideas. Normally when we have conversations with others we base our statements off of our own experiences and ideas. This structure follows that same vein of thought. An example of this could be a speech arguing that all students should be required to take a foreign language in college in order to be more culturally educated citizens.

Argument of Policy

The third type of argument you can make is a claim of policy. This means you are calling for an action to be taken or that we should or ought to do something. This is a very common structure used by politicians or activists who are calling for an element of change to occur. An example of this could be a speech arguing that there should be free parking throughout Athens on weekends since the area around campus is so busy on Friday and Saturday nights.

CONCLUSION

This chapter focused on the key elements of Toulmin's (1958) model of argument and provided discussion about how the model will be beneficial to you not only in COMS 1030, but also in your personal and professional life. Public speaking is a skill that is developed over an extended period of practice and experience, and COMS 1030 serves as a starting point for you on the journey to being a confident and polished speaker. By understanding Toulmin's (1958) model and knowing how to use the elements to assist you in stating and supporting your ideas, the process to become a better public speaker, who can clearly articulate and support their views and beliefs, should be an easier process that you will hopefully enjoy.

REFERENCES

Toulmin, S. (2001). *Return to reason*. Cambridge, NY: Harvard University Press.

Toulmin, S. (1958). *The uses of argument*. Cambridge, NY: Cambridge University Press.

Walton, D. (2005). *Fundamentals of critical argumentation*. Cambridge, NY: Cambridge University Press.

Chapter 15 PERSUASIVE SPEECH ASSIGNMENT

BY LAURA BLACK AND JESSICA FURGERSON*

*Annette N. Hamel, Brian M. Swafford, and Dan West contributed to previous versions of this chapter.

PERSUASIVE SPEECH ASSIGNMENT

Your final major assignment for this class is a persuasive speech. Persuasion is about inducing change, and in your persuasive speech you will try to change your audience members' beliefs or behaviors in some way. This sounds daunting, and persuasion can take a lot of practice. However, you encounter persuasion in your everyday life and can probably think of many situations where you have tried to persuade a friend, family member, coworker, or teacher to believe you or do something for you. Persuading others is an inherently ethical task—it is easy to think about situations where politicians or advertisers are disingenuous about their motivations or the true consequences of the change they are asking for. As you craft your persuasive messages we encourage you to seriously reflect on the ethical dimensions of the change you are promoting.

> General Purpose: To persuade
>
> Time: 6–8 minutes
>
> Requires research—Minimum of 5 appropriate sources
>
> One to three notecards allowed
>
> **ASSIGNMENT HIGHLIGHTS**

SELECTING A TOPIC

When it comes time to select your topic, you should consider what you want your audience to do and what arguments you are going to use to convince them of your position. As you select your topic, there are some important things that you must consider.

First, you must ask yourself if the topic you have selected is *controversial*. A controversial topic is important for a persuasive presentation because it ensures that there is more than one side to the issue and that the audience could be persuaded. Topics like dieting or exercise are not considered controversial because we all know that we should eat properly and exercise. So there is no debate and the audience is not likely to be persuaded. Controversial topics like rising tuition on college campuses or reducing our reliance on non-renewable energy sources could be excellent examples of good persuasive topics. Topics like abortion, gay marriage, and gun control are all very controversial and have very diverse positions, but often make for poor persuasive speech topics because they represent salient beliefs.

Salient beliefs are those beliefs that a person strongly holds. A person will likely already have an opinion for topics like gun control, gay marriage, and abortion. As a speaker, it is important to realize that you cannot change someone's salient beliefs in a short amount of time. Instead, when picking a persuasive topic, try to get your audience to make a small, incremental change.

A persuasive presentation must also have a topic that has *new arguments*. When we consider issues like abortion or gun control, we see that the arguments used to support those sides have been around for decades. Instead of using these topics, look for controversial topics with new arguments. Topics like illegally downloading music, steroids in sports, heightened security in airports over the past ten years, or using refillable water bottles instead of plastic bottles are all topics with new arguments that the audience might not have been exposed to previously.

In addition to topic selection, you must also *consider your audience*. They will have bearing on what topics would be considered controversial. For example, on a college campus, a speech about lowering the legal drinking age from 21 to 18 would not be considered controversial. In fact, you might get a standing ovation from your classmates. But, that same speech would be highly controversial if given at a meeting of the Mothers Against Drunk Driving (MADD). As you brainstorm topics, think about the audience that will hear your speech and their views on whatever issue you select.

WRITING A PROPOSITION

A persuasive speech utilizes a proposition rather than a thesis statement. A proposition *proposes a change* in the audience's attitudes, actions, or beliefs. Once you have selected a topic, you will write your general purpose and your specific purpose statements. Your textbook uses the phrase "My audience will ..." to help you craft your specific purpose statement. An example of a specific purpose statement might be, "My audience will stop using plastic water bottles." Once you have your specific purpose statement, you are ready to write your proposition.

A good proposition has three components: An agent of action, the word "should," and the desired outcome.

1 | The Agent of Action

A good persuasive speech must specify who is supposed to be the one to act. This actor is called the agent of action. The agent of action can be the audience, the government, or some other entity that is in a position to act. It is important for you to consider what the agent of action is capable of doing. For example, if you are talking about changing state regulations about energy production, college students in the classroom are not able to take any action on the topic. Instead, that speech should be directed at the state government that is in charge of setting those regulations.

2 | The Word "Should"

"Should" is an action word that gives your proposition focus. You are telling your audience what action they should take. Additionally, "should" is different than words like "might" or "could." If the proposition says that some action might be taken or could be taken, it implies that the action might not be taken. Instead, your proposition should be definitive and tell the audience exactly what you want them to do.

3 | The Desired Outcome

This portion of your proposition should come directly from your specific purpose statement. You have already written down what your audience will do after your speech. That is the desired outcome. So you will simply write down that desired outcome here in your proposition. Back to the energy topic, you would say, "The state of Ohio should give tax incentives to companies who use solar, wind, and other renewable energy sources."

ORGANIZATIONAL PATTERNS

Once you have a topic and have done some research to support that topic, you must organize your persuasive speech. But the organization is not as simple as just standing up and making a series of arguments in some random order. As noted earlier, your audience may have some preconceived notions about your topic. It is important for you to organize your persuasive presentation in such a way as to maximize the likelihood of audience compliance. To that end, here are three organization patterns for your persuasive speech and how each might be best suited for a particular audience.

1 | Problem-Cause-Solution Pattern

In a problem-cause-solution pattern, you will establish a problem, explain the causes for that problem, and offer a solution. As a result, the pattern is organized around three main points: (1) There is a problem that requires action. (2) The cause for the problem is preventing change. (3) There is a solution to overcome the cause and solve the problem. This pattern also works well for topics where the audience is unfamiliar with the problem, has no opinion, or is only mildly in favor of or opposed to the topic.

Topic: Plastic Bottle Waste

General Purpose: To Persuade

Specific Purpose: My audience will stop buying bottled water.

Proposition: You should use a refillable bottle instead of buying disposable water bottles.

Main Points:
    I.   Disposable bottles cost billions of dollars, fill our landfills, and harm the environment. (The statement of the problem)

    II.   The bottled water industry and society's apathy to change have prevented action. (Cause of the problem)

    III.   People should refill their bottles with tap water instead of buying disposable bottles. (Solution to the problem)

2 | Statement of Logical Reasons Pattern

In this organizational pattern, you will present the best-supported reasons for agreeing with your position. For this organizational pattern, you will have your second-strongest reason first, your strongest reason last and any other reasons in the middle. This is so you start off with a strong reason. You'll build your argument by listing other reasons, then end with a "bang" by stating your strongest, most important reason last. This pattern works best when your audience has no opinion on the subject, is apathetic, or only mildly supports or dislikes.

Topic: Becoming a volunteer.

General Purpose: To Persuade

Specific Purpose: My audience will learn why they should volunteer in their communities.

Proposition: You should volunteer in your community.

Main Points:

    I.   Volunteers are needed to help community organizations run smoothly. (Second strongest reason)

    II.   Volunteering looks great on your resume. (Other reason)

    III.   It is simple and easy to volunteer in your community. (Strongest reason)

Speech Outline

In the pages that follow you will see a sample persuasive speech outline created by COMS 1030 student Brittany Swint. Notice that her speech uses a statement of logical reasons pattern to support her proposition that everyone who is eligible to donate blood should do so.

Brittany Swint
Formal Sentence Outline
COMS 1030

Title of Speech: Blood Donation
Specific Purpose: My audience will donate blood.
Proposition: Everyone who is eligible for blood donation should give blood.

SAMPLE | FORMAL SENTENCE
OUTLINE (PERSUASIVE)

Introduction

I. Attention Getter

If you could save a total of three lives in ten minutes would you do it? By giving one pint of blood, you could do just that.

II. Audience Relevance Link:

Though many of us have not been in a situation where we needed a blood transfusion; we could at any time be in a circumstance where that is the case. If others are willing to give their blood to help us, we should be able to return the favor. It also feels great to know you are helping someone else.

III. Credibility

My family members are all Jehovah's Witnesses. Their religion does not permit them to receive blood transfusions. Every summer, my sister and I would visit them. While in their care, we would not be able to receive blood transfusions because of their religion's restrictions unless my parents had signed a letter saying they permitted them. I don't want to restrict the amount of people who can accept blood transfusions; I want to increase it, which explains why I have donated blood.

IV. Proposition

Everyone who is eligible for blood donation should give blood.

V. Preview

The benefits of giving blood are endless. First, it doesn't hurt our own health, second, it's easy and third, you can become someone else's hero in just a short period of time.

Transition: While donating blood can be a scary experience, it is not detrimental to our health in any way because our blood is plentiful and it can help to boost our health.

Body

I. Contrary to popular belief, giving blood can actually benefit our own bodies.

   A. Giving blood is not harmful because we have so much of it.

      1. The American Red Cross's website states that with the abundance of blood in our systems, we have plenty of it to share (Donating Blood, 2011).

      2. The website also clarifies that with the high amount of blood, it is disappointing that there is so little to go around (Donating Blood, 2011).

B. Donating blood can actually increase our health.

   1. Alvear, the author for *CNN.com Health,* provided evidence that giving blood lowers the blood iron levels. High iron in the blood contributes to cardiovascular disease since it increases the oxidation process of cholesterol in the body (Alvear, 2000).

   2. According to the Livestrong website, donating blood has been known to show a decrease in the risk of getting certain cancers and can reduce the chance of getting a heart attack by 88% (Schuna, 2011).

   3. Every time that you donate blood, your body replenishes the blood that was lost within 48 hours. This replenishment can help your body work more efficiently because the new red blood cells are ready to transport more oxygen as previously cited (Schuna, 2011).

   4. The journal, *Heart and Education* claims that donating blood can also show a reduction in cardiovascular events such as strokes, high blood pressure, and coronary artery diseases (Meyer, 2011).

Transition: Giving blood is not only beneficial; it's easy to do.

II. Donating blood is a relatively simple process because of two reasons.

   A. The first reason that donating blood is easy is because there are only a few guidelines to follow to ensure that the donating process runs smoothly.

      1. The American Red Cross says by keeping hydrated, wearing something comfortable, and consuming iron-rich foods, you will be more relaxed, and decrease your chances of fainting (Donating Blood, 2011).

   B. The second reason that donating blood is easy is because there are only four discrete steps you must follow in order to give blood.

      1. The first step is registration where you will sign in, present a form of identification, and go over eligibility requirements (Donating Blood, 2011).

      2. The second step is a mini-physical where your blood pressure, pulse, and hemoglobin levels will be tested (Donating Blood, 2011).

      3. The third step is the donation itself. Your arm will be cleaned and a needle will be inserted quickly. After a pint is collected, the professional will remove the needle and bandage the arm (Donating Blood, 2011).

      4. The fourth step is my personal favorite. This is the refreshment stage where everyone can enjoy snacks such as cookies and crackers and get something to drink. All of these steps were explained thoroughly by the American Red Cross (Donating Blood, 2011).

Transition: Donating blood is so simple, but there are not enough people that do it, resulting in fewer lives being saved.

III. Donating blood can make you someone else's hero.

   A. Donating blood saves lives.

1. One pint of blood can save three lives as said by "America's Blood Centers" (Blood Donation, 2011).

2. As previously cited, blood is always needed for someone. Accident victims, cancer patients, hemophiliacs, premature infants, and often surgery patients who are receiving transplants need at least some type of blood transfusion. Anemic patients require blood transfusions of red blood cells to stay alive (Blood Donation, 2011).

3. Blood transfusions are needed for people with blood diseases such as sickle cell anemia (Blood Donation, 2011).

4. Finally, the American Red Cross sadly asserts that people receiving organ transplants are often refused organs because there is no blood available to them during the time of the transplant (Donating Blood, 2011).

Transition: Giving blood is the easiest way to say; "I saved someone's life today."

Conclusion

I. Review Main Points

I have explained to you the extraordinary benefits of donating blood. Donating blood is beneficial to our health, it is an easy process, and it can make you a hero in theory and reality.

II. Restate Proposition

Everyone that is eligible to donate blood should give blood.

III. Decisive Closing

There are not enough people donating blood in the world today. This is a problem with a modest solution. Donating blood helps us and it helps others, too. A ten-minute process can save up to three lives. In the six minutes that I have presented, at least 720 people in America needed a blood transfusion. We have the opportunity to be someone else's hero. We can give someone else the chance to have another smile, another hug, another laugh, and the best yet, another chance at life.

References

Alvear, M. (2000). Evidence suggests that giving blood has health benefits. *CNN.com Health*. Retrieved from http://archives.cnn.com/2000/HEALTH/04/26/give.blood.wmd/

Blood Donation. (2011). *America's Blood Centers: It's about life*. Retrieved from http://www.americasblood.org/go.cfm?do=Page.View&pid=5

Donating Blood. (2011). *American National Red Cross*. Retrieved from http://www.redcrossblood.org/donating-blood/donation-process

Meyer, D.G., Strickland, D., Maloley, P.A., Seburg, J. J., Wilson, J.E., & McManus, B.F. (2011). Possible association of a reduction in cardiovascular events with blood donation. *HEART and education in heart*. Vol 78, Issue 2. Retrieved from http://heart.bmj.com/content/78/2/188.full.pdf

Schuna, Carly. (2011). Health Benefits of Donating Blood. *Livestrong: The limitless potential of you*. Retrieved from http://www.livestrong.com/article/96891-health-benefits-donating- blood

PEER EVALUATION OF PERSUASIVE SPEECH ASSIGNMENT

Your Name: _____

Speaker's Name: _____ Topic: _____

Use this legend to understand the quality of your classmate's performance in each category.

"+" Well Done   "o" Okay/Average   " – " Needs Improvement   "×" Not Included

_____ **Introduction**

    _____ Attention getter
    _____ Established relevance
    _____ Established credibility
    _____ Clear thesis statement
    _____ Included preview

_____ **Body**

    _____ Effective organization
    _____ Support/evidence
    _____ Clear transitions

_____ **Conclusion**

    _____ Reviewed main points
    _____ Restated thesis statement
    _____ Ended speech strongly

_____ **Delivery**

    _____ Effective vocal delivery
    _____ Used hand gestures well
    _____ Maintained eye contact
    _____ Used extemporaneous style
    _____ Used notecards effectively

Written Comments

Three Things the Speaker did Well:

Three Things to Improve:

CRITERIA FOR EVALUATING PERSUASIVE SPEECHES

Introduction 15 Points Possible

Gained Attention	**(C)** = Prepared audience to listen **(B)** = and creates a need to listen **(A)** = and is original & creative.
Made Topic Relevant	**(C)** = Established importance of topic **(B)** = and relates the topic to audience **(A)** = and is significant to the audience.
Established Credibility	**(C)** = Student states why she/he is credible to speak on the topic **(B)** = and is a logical argument for the speaker **(A)** = and is unique & creative.
Stated Thesis Clearly	**(C)** = Statement is clear & direct **(B)** = and it flows logically to the preview **(A)** = and it reflects a unique & creative approach to the topic.
Stated Preview Clearly	**(C)** = Statement outlines main points **(B)** = and flows from the thesis **(A)** = and uses original and creative language.

Body 30 Points Possible

Main Points Clear	**(C)** = Main points are easily identifiable **(B)** = and each main point is an independent idea **(A)** = and main points are set-up previews and signposts.
Strong Evidence & Support	**(C)** = Minimum of 5 sources are orally cited **(B)** = and links between sources and main points are clear **(A)** = and there is evidence of persuasive analysis and understanding.
Organization Effective	**(C)** = Issue is appropriate for audience **(B)** = and meets the needs of the audience **(A)**= and is clearly constructed with persuasive language.
Used Precise, Clear, & Descriptive Language	**(C)** = Language is appropriate **(B)** = and language is predominantly concrete, **(A)** = and language is vivid, creative, and utilizes imagery or metaphors.

Conclusion 10 Points Possible

Restated Thesis	**(C)** = Thesis is clearly stated **(B)** = and flows with a transition from the body of the speech **(A)** = and flows with a transition to the review of main points.
Reviewed Main Points	**(C)** = Briefly reviewed all main points **(B)** = and transitions are used **(A)** = and it is different from the preview statement in the introduction.
Made Presentation Memorable	**(C)** = Topic was adapted to audience **(B)** = and the speech made references to the audience **(A)** = and the speech considered the audience's thinking about the topic.

Delivery 20 Points Possible

Used Vocal Variety	**(C)** = Some vocal variety used during parts of the speech **(B)** = and vocal variety is used to highlight ideas **(A)** = and the speaker uses voice, rate, and diction to demonstrate interest in the speech.
Used Appropriate Articulation/ Pronunciation	**(C)** = There are 3 or more mis-articulated or mispronounced words. **(B)** = There are 3 or fewer mis-articulated or mispronounced correctly. **(A)** = All words are articulated and pronounced correctly.
Established Eye Contact With the Audience	**(C)** = Maintained eye contact with the audience **(B)** = and the student is able to move between looking at the audience and the notecard **(A)** = and gages feedback from the audience for a majority of the time.
Used Appropriate Gestures, Body Movement, & Facial Expressions	**(C)** = Some distracting gestures, body movement or facial expressions. **(B)** = Gestures, body movement, and facial expressions add emphasis. **(A)** = Gestures, body movement, and facial expressions are used to demonstrate enthusiasm for the speech.

Use the following notations to evaluate your classmate's speech:
"+" Well Done   "o" Okay/Average   " – " Needs Improvement   "×" Not Included

INSTRUCTOR EVALUATION OF PERSUASIVE SPEECH ASSIGNMENT

Speaker's Name: _____   Total Points: _____ /100

Time Infraction: _____   Time: _____

Use this legend to understand the quality of your performance in each category.

"+" Well Done   "o" Okay/Average   " – " Needs Improvement   "×" Not Included

_____ **Introduction   (10 points)**

_____ Gained attention
_____ Made topic relevant
_____ Established credibility
_____ Stated thesis clearly
_____ Stated preview clearly

_____ **Body   (30 points)**

_____ Proved existence of issue with evidence and reasoning
_____ Clearly connected intended audience to issue with evidence and reasoning
_____ Quality of main points of argument development
_____ Used precise, clear, and descriptive language
_____ Speech was persuasive in nature

_____ **Conclusion   (10 points)**

_____ Restated proposition
_____ Summarized thesis and reviewed main points
_____ Clear, achievable action step
_____ Made presentation memorable

_____ **Organization   (5 points)**

_____ Main points organized in proper sequence building to action
_____ Main points broken down into sub-points
_____ Organized well (transitions, internal summaries, flows well)
_____ Main points were developed evenly

_____ **Supporting Material   (5 points)**

_____ Quality of supporting material (examples, statistics, quotations)
_____ Appropriate sources
_____ Cited at least five appropriate sources

Speeches have a 15 second grace period over/under time limit without penalty. Speeches that go 16–29 seconds over/under the time limit will be reduced by 3 points. Speeches that go 30 seconds over/under the time limit will be reduced by 5 points. Excessive time infraction can result in larger penalty per discretion of Instructor.

_____ **Delivery** **(30 points)**

_____ Used vocal variety
_____ Used appropriate articulation/pronunciation
_____ Used minimal vocal disfluencies
_____ Established eye contact with audience
_____ Used appropriate gestures and body movement, facial expressions
_____ Appropriate pitch, rate, volume

_____ **Outline and References** **(10 points)**

_____ Narrowed and focused
_____ Reflected presentation
_____ Used proper outline format (including transitions, full sentence structure, and correct grammar and spelling)
_____ Credibility of sources
_____ At least five sources included in bibliography
_____ Sources cited throughout the outline in APA Format
_____ References in APA format
_____ Submitted to safe-assign

Presentation Strengths:

Areas for Improvement:

Chapter 16 IMPROMPTU JOB INTERVIEW SPEECH ASSIGNMENT

BY KEITH C. BISTODEAU

IMPROMPTU JOB INTERVIEW SPEECH ASSIGNMENT

ASSIGNMENT RATIONALE

Participating in a job interview is often an intimidating and exciting experience. This assignment is meant to help you practice for two key aspects of the job interview: crafting/defending your resume and answering job interview questions. As a result of this assignment you will develop a resume, practice impromptu speaking, and improve critical listening skills.

Time limit: 4–6 minutes

Impromptu Delivery Mode

One notecard allowed

ASSIGNMENT HIGHLIGHTS

ASSIGNMENT OVERVIEW

This assignment requires you to prepare a resume for an internship or summer job during college or perhaps a job you would like to attain upon graduating from college. You will prepare responses to several common interview questions, and present your responses in a simulated interview with your Instructor in front of the class.

ASSIGNMENT COMPONENTS

For any job interview you must fill out a resume/application and complete an interview. For this assignment there are two components you must complete: the creation of a resume, and a simulated job interview. To better understand why these two elements are included in this assignment, they are explained in more detail below.

RESUME

The resume is the first document that a potential employer receives from you. Hence, this is your first opportunity to demonstrate your competence and ability to meet their needs. A strong resume has the following components:

☐ A clean and easy to follow layout

☐ Clearly labeled contact information

☐ A clear statement about the position you are interested in

☐ Well-structured sections

- Statement of intent
- Education history
- Employment history
- Awards/certifications
- Other job related skills

For help creating your resume, review the important information provided by OU's Career and Leadership Development Center's (CLDC) advice on resume writing. You can access their Job Search Guide here: *http://www.ohio.edu/careerandleadership/upload/job_search_guide_final-2.pdf*. Specifically pages 24–25 address how to write a resume, contain various resume formats, and provide sample resumes. You should also review the OCLDC's Resume Checklist here *http://www.ohio.edu/careerandleadership/upload/CLDC-Resume-Checklist.pdf* (note this checklist discusses what you need to do to upload your resume to Bobcat Career Links, you do not need to do that for this assignment, but the suggestions they provide are useful).

IMPROMPTU INTERVIEW

After you submit your resume, if the company you are applying to likes what they see, they may invite you to participate in an interview. Oftentimes this part of the job search process is rife with uncertainty because you do not know the specific questions that a potential employer may ask you. To help you prepare for the interview, you will find a list of sample interview questions below that you can use for practice. The list below may contain questions your Instructor uses in the simulated interview, or will be similar to the type of questions that you will be asked during the interview portion of the assignment.

The goal of this part of the assignment is to simulate a brief interview situation. You will be asked to bring in a copy of your resume to your Instructor, and will be asked questions based off your resume and the particular job you are interested in. To make this easier for your Instructor and for yourself you should either bring in a job ad, or create a job ad for a position you are interested in applying for either now or in the future.

What to Bring to Class on the Day of the Impromptu Interview

- Resume
- Job Description/Job Call
- Yourself

Potential Interview Questions

- Why are you interested in working for this company?
- Why are you interested in this position?
- Why do you feel you are qualified for this position?
- What skills or training have you had that will help you with the job responsibilities for this position?
- What is the most difficult job situation you have faced?
  - How did you handle it?
- What are you looking for in a job?
- Do you work better in a team or on your own?
- Do you have any questions about the company?

INSTRUCTOR EVALUATION OF IMPROMPTU JOB INTERVIEW SPEECH ASSIGNMENT

Speaker's Name: _____ Total Points: _____ /50

Time Infraction: _____ Time: _____

Use this legend to understand the quality of your performance in each category.

"+" Well Done   "o" Okay/Average   " – " Needs Improvement   "×" Not Included

_____ **Resume** **(20 points)**

_____ /5 All components of the resume are included and an attempt to include suggestions from OU's CLDC are evident.

_____ /10 Thoroughness of resume sections

_____ /5 Proper spelling and grammar

_____ **Impromptu Interview** **(10 points)**

_____ Clear, appropriate, and thorough answers are provided

_____ **Delivery** **(20 points)**

_____ Used vocal variety

_____ Used appropriate articulation/pronunciation

_____ Used minimal vocal disfluencies

_____ Established eye contact with audience

_____ Used appropriate gestures and body movement, facial expressions

_____ Appropriate pitch, rate, volume

Overall Feedback:

Speeches have a 15 second grace period over/under time limit without penalty. Speeches that go 16–29 seconds over/under the time limit will be reduced by 3 points. Speeches that go 30 seconds over/under the time limit will be reduced by 5 points. Excessive time infraction can result in larger penalty per discretion of Instructor.

Chapter 17 SPEAKING TIPS AND DRILLS

BY KEITH C. BISTODEAU

SPEAKING TIPS AND DRILLS

The following tips and tricks are meant to serve as a guide for you to improve as a speaker. These activities are used to promote public speaking success by the author and the Ohio University Speaking Bobcats. All of these tips and drills can be done in less than 1 minute (meaning you could do all of these in under 15 minutes). Try them at home, between classes, or right before your next speech. You may be surprised by how much of a difference you notice.

TIP 1: ALWAYS KEEP YOUR JAW/MOUTH RELAXED

Name of Drill: The Jaw Drop

Purpose of the Drill: When your mouth is relaxed your whole face is relaxed. This makes you appear more comfortable when speaking in front of an audience.

This drill focuses on having you drop your jaw as much as possible while speaking. The point of this is to allow you to have your voice project clearly to the audience. To complete this drill you must have a copy of your speech in front of you. If you do not have a copy of you speech you can practice this drill by reading your textbook.

Steps in the Drill:

- Read a passage normally for thirty seconds.
- Now re-read the same part dropping your jaw as low as possible.
- Finally, re-read the same passage. You should notice a big difference from the first time you read the document.
- Repeat as necessary for practice.

TIP 2: MAINTAIN GOOD EYE CONTACT

Name of the Drill: The Gaze

Purpose of the Drill: Maintaining eye contact shows confidence and helps to establish credibility. This drill focuses on keeping strong eye contact with your audience. Professional speakers are trained not to look away from their audience because eye contact symbolizes confidence, power, and intelligence.

Steps in the Drill:

- To complete this drill you will need a partner.
- You will take turns speaking with a partner.
- While you are speaking you are not to break eye contact with your partner.
- While you are speaking your partner will try to get you to break eye contact.
- After this drill is complete you should have a better grasp of how to maintain eye contact while speaking, even when distractions occur.
- Repeat as necessary for practice.

TIP 3: REMEMBER TO BREATHE

Name of the Drill: Alphabet Olympics

Purpose of the Drill: You need air to be able to project and for your body to relax.

This drill focuses on training your body to consistently breathe while giving speeches. All you need for this drill is a stopwatch or clock.

Steps in the Drill:

- To complete this drill you will need to alternate between saying the alphabet as fast as you can in one breath, and saying the alphabet as slow as you can while taking a breath after each letter.
- This drill helps you focus on how breathing changes your pace while speaking and can help you not only emphasize key points, but also help your body relax.
- Repeat as necessary for practice.

TIP 4: KEEP YOUR HANDS WHERE YOU CAN SEE THEM

Name of the Drill: Magnetic Hands

Purpose of the Drill: Hand gestures below the waist are awkward and distracting.

This drill focuses on allowing you to be aware of the distracting nonverbal gestures you may make while speaking. All you need for this drill is a mirror. This drill trains your body to respond to subconscious messages that control your movements.

Steps in the Drill:
- While standing in front of the mirror hold your hands in front of you about one foot apart.
- While looking at the mirror repeat "attract" slowly and clearly over and over.
- You will notice that your hands will slowly move together.
- Once your hands touch, shake them out and rest them level with your waist.
- Once near your waist say "repel" over and over and focus on raising your arms slowly.
- These two actions will subtly train your brain to not only keep your hands centered on your body, but also above your waist.
- This will help you have a more open, relaxed, and inviting body posture while speaking.
- Repeat as necessary for practice.

TIP 5: DON'T ROCK THE BOAT (I.E., YOUR BODY)

Name of the Drill: Left-Right-Left

Purpose of the Drill: You want your audience to focus on your words, not how you shift your body. This drill focuses on staying in one place while speaking. This drill is not intended to remove movement, but to ensure all the movement is purposeful so you don't look like you are nervous while speaking.

Steps in the Drill:
- To do this drill you need to repeat a simple phrase over and over in your head for about a minute (e.g., "when life gives you lemons make lemonade").
- Once you have done this you need to stand up and march in place while saying the phrase out loud.
- Once you have done this for a little while try to say the phrase in the military cadence pattern for marching.
- This helps to train your brain to associate your movement with a specific goal.
- By doing this, when you prepare speeches your body will only be draw to move when you are making an impactful statement or when your body needs to move to relax.
- This will help to limit your movement while adding poise to your delivery and style.
- Repeat as necessary for practice.

TIP 6: KEEP A FIRM BASE

Name of the Drill: Cement Shoes

Purpose of the Drill: Just like a house, a firm foundation leads to a better structure and frame. This drill focuses on making sure you do not move your feet while speaking. You can do this with a partner or alone.

Steps in the Drill:

- To start you must place your feet right next to one another and lock them in place (if you have a partner let them hold your feet).
- Then you need to start speaking and try not to focus on your feet.
- If you try to move you should be able to feel the resistance against your feet.
- Now repeat this drill again with your feet shoulder width apart.
- You should notice how much more relaxed your body is and how much less your body wants to move.
- This is because having your feet placed roughly shoulder width apart is a natural resting position for the body.
- Repeat as necessary for practice.

TIP 7: MOVEMENT CAN BE A GOOD THING

Name of the Drill: Mime Time

Purpose of the Drill: You don't need to be stiff like a board, just not wet like a noodle.

This drill will teach you how to use your body to help represent what you are trying to say. You can do this with a partner or a group.

Steps in the Drill:

- What you need to do is write out a list of simple actions and cut up the slips of paper and put them into a bowl.
- Then you take turns drawing slips and acting out the actions.
- You can give no hints and you can only stop once your partner or the group guesses what you are doing.
- This not only helps you better understand the power of words, but also helps you better understand how words and movements work together.
- Repeat as necessary for practice.

TIP 8: PACE MATTERS

Name of the Drill: Time to Race

Purpose of the Drill: You are not an auctioneer, so just have a conversation. This drill will help you focus on staying conversational while speaking. For this drill you will need a partner.

Steps in the Drill:

- What you need to do is write out a list of five simple sentences.
- Then you both need to hold the list in front of you and start to read the list aloud at the same time.
- Once you get comfortable with the list you need to try and go faster than your partner.
- Keep doing this until one of you gives up or until it becomes too fast to understand what is being said.
- This drill will help you not rush while you are speaking.
- Repeat as necessary for practice.

TIP 9: VOLUME MATTERS

Name of the Drill: Silence is Not Golden

Purpose of the Drill: Too loud or too little and your message is lost.

This drill will help you train your brain to pick up on pauses during your natural speech. You need to have a copy of your speech.

Steps in the Drill:

- What you need to do is to try and give the speech from memory as best you can.
- Anytime you stop you need to start over, but you must give the speech louder than you did before.
- Do this 3–4 times, and then repeat the process by getting quieter each time you stop.
- This will not only help you with memory, but will also help you gauge how loud you need to speak to have the proper volume in a room.
- Repeat as necessary for practice.

TIP 10: DICTION/CLARITY MATTERS

Name of the Drill: Lips, Tongue, and Teeth

Purpose of the Drill: This will add confidence and make you more believable. This drill will help you train your tongue, mouth, and jaw to be stronger and more easily controlled while speaking.

Steps in the Drill:

- The goal here is to repeat a phrase as quickly and clearly as possible.
- The phrase is "The lips, the tip of the tongue, the teeth, the lips, the tip of the tongue."
- Start out saying this slowly and then slowly say it faster and faster.
- This is a phrase that uses all of your mouth and will train you to use your jaw efficiently so it will not become tired while speaking.
- This will reduce verbal clutter and the slurring/dropping of words.
- Repeat as necessary for practice.

WHAT STUDENTS SAY ABOUT THESE TIPS AND DRILLS

Students who have used these tips and drills when preparing for their speeches have said they not only felt more comfortable giving speeches, but also felt more prepared. These tips and drills will allow you to have more practice before you give your speech in class and they also help you subtly train your brain and body to be relaxed while giving speeches. The more you do these drills, the easier they will become, and the more comfortable you will be speaking in front an audience.

Chapter 18 COMMUNICATION RESOURCE CENTER INFORMATION

COMMUNICATION RESOURCE CENTER INFORMATION — QUICK REFERENCE GUIDE

The following handout walks you through the basics of the Communication Resource Center (CRC). Please consult this reference guide before and after your appointment time for important details about your obligations at the CRC to receive course credit.

WHAT IS THE CRC?

The mission of the Communication Resource Center (CRC) is to help students at Ohio University enrolled in COMS 1030 enhance their public speaking skills in a positive, friendly, and safe environment. The goals of the CRC are to (1) provide an environment in which students enrolled in COMS1030 can practice and enhance skills developed in the course and (2) to help students develop and grow into confident and competent communicators. The CRC is a unique resource afforded to you as a COMS 1030 student that allows you to get help selecting a topic, preparing your outlines, assistance with research, and practice your speech in a low-risk environment prior to your in-class speech. During this time you will practice your speech one-on-one with trained CRC Peer Leaders who have all completed, and excelled in COMS 1030.

STEP 1: MAKING YOUR APPOINTMENT

- You will schedule all appointments at the following website: *www.comsspeechlab.appointy.com*. Please note that this is an external website, separate from OU. You will need to sign-up for a unique username and password that is separate from your OU credentials.
- Each appointment time is 20 minutes in length.
- It is imperative you schedule your appointment **at least 24 hours** in advance of your in-class speech day.
- If you need to cancel an appointment, it is important that you do so within **24 hours** of your scheduled appointment time. To cancel an appointment, login to you Appointy account and click "cancel appointment."
- We plan to offer walk walk in hours and extended hours during major speech assignments.

STEP 2: DURING YOUR APPOINTMENT

- Please arrive at least **five** minutes before your appointment time to prevent delays.

- The CRC is located on the bottom floor of the Schoonover Center (SCHN 030). Please make sure you are familiar with this location prior to your appointment time. If you are unsure of the location, please consult your Instructor or e-mail speechlab@ohio.edu.

- On the day of your appointment you should bring any materials you need with you to work on your speech. If you plan to practice your speech you should bring an outline with you.

- When you arrive for your appointment, a CRC Peer Leader will greet you and you will begin working with them.

STEP 3: AFTER YOUR APPOINTMENT

- After the completion of your CRC visit, your CRC Leader will provide you with a *pink* sheet that will contain the Peer Leader's feedback and signature. It is imperative you keep this pink sheet and turn it in to your Instructor within **48 hours** of your CRC visit. This is the only way you will receive credit for your participation. We encourage you to return to the CRC as many times as you want, but you can only receive credit once.

- If you practice your entire speech, you will be e-mailed a copy of your speech performance. This is an important resource. Please review your video to help you practice before your in-class speech.

COMS 3920 · COMMUNICATION RESOURCE CENTER (CRC) PRACTICUM

COURSE OBJECTIVE

The Communication Resource Center (CRC) is a resource available to all undergraduate COMS students. Our mission is to help students at Ohio University enrolled in COMS 1030 enhance their public speaking skills in a positive, friendly, and safe environment.

COURSE DESCRIPTION

This three-hour practicum will provide undergraduate students with experience in the areas of training, development, assessment, and instruction. In conjunction with the Communication Resource Center (CRC) coordinator, CRC Peer Leaders will do the following:

> Upon successfully completing COMS 1030 you can help train and mentor your peers. You would enroll in COMS 3920 (course description on this page) and engage in service hours in the CRC. If you are interested, complete the CRC Peer Leader Applicaiton form on the following pages.
>
> **BECOME A COMS CRC PEER LEADER!**

1 | Semester Training: Meet during the first month of the semester to engage in training that will focus on developing undergraduate students' skills to run and operate the CRC and become a peer leader. This will included being trained to provide feedback to peers on presentation related activities.

2 | CRC Hours: After completing the month-long training course, CRC Peer Leaders will work a total of three hours a week assisting students by providing feedback, assessing, and tutoring students enrolled in COMS 1030 Fundamentals of Public Speaking.

Specific duties and tasks for students enrolled in the practicum may include:

- Listening to student speeches
- Providing feedback to students
- Aiding students in brainstorming topic ideas
- Providing assistance in writing speeches
- Assisting students in speech delivery

3 | Monthly Meetings: After the initial training training students will meet with the CRC Coordinator for monthly meetings to discuss progress and answer questions.

The CRC Coordinator will provide you with a schedule of meetings at the beginning of the semester.

4 | Reflections: Students' will produce two written (3–4 pages) reflections about their experience as CRC Peer Leaders.

PREREQUISITES FOR THE COURSE

- Student must have completed COMS 1030 and earned at least a B or higher
- Student must complete the CRC Undergraduate Mentor Application, that includes:
    - Complete Application Information Sheet
    - Referral from COMS 1030 Instructor
- Statement expressing rationale for becoming a CRC Peer Leader
    - Copy Resume
- Hold a cumulative GPA of 3.0 or higher

COMS 3920 — COMMUNICATION RESOURCE CENTER (CRC) PEER LEADER APPLICATION

Due Date: Last Friday of regularly scheduled classes before the final exam period begins.

Demographic Information

Name:

Year in School:

E-mail Address:

Grade Earned/Anticipated in COMS 1030:

Please list the name of your COMS 1030 Instructor:

Skills or Qualifications

Summarize knowledge, skills, and abilities that prepare you for this position:

Rationale for Application

Summarize your rationale for applying to be a CRC Peer Leader:

COMS Recommendation

Please request a recommendation from your COMS Instructor. Your Instructor should describe your knowledge and abilities that prepare you to train and mentor future COMS 1030 students. If you have already taken COMS 1030, we prefer your recommendation come from your COMS 1030 Instructor but we will accept another COMS faculty member's letter of recommendation. Your Instructor should utilize the space provided below or attach additional pages, as needed.

Thank you for completing this application form and for your interest in a CRC Peer Leader position. Please also include a pdf copy of your resume and submit all materials electronically to Rachel Presley, CRC Coordinator (rp144015@ohio.edu) by the due date listed on the first page. Questions and concerns should be directed to Dr. Angela Hosek (hosek@ohio.edu). You will be notified via email about the status of your application. If accepted, you will need to enroll in COMS 3920 with the CRC Coordinator.